Annual Reviews Monograph

INTELLIGENCE AND AFFECTIVITY:
Their Relationship During Child Development

by Jean Piaget

Translated and Edited by T. A. Brown and C. E. Kaegi
Illinois State Psychiatric Institute, Chicago

Consulting Editor, Mark R. Rosenzweig
University of California, Berkeley

ANNUAL REVIEWS INC.   4139 EL CAMINO WAY   PALO ALTO, CALIFORNIA 94306 USA

R ANNUAL REVIEWS INC.
Palo Alto, California, USA

International Standard Book Number: 0-8243-2901-5
Library of Congress Catalog Card Number: 80-70760

PRINTED AND BOUND IN THE UNITED STATES OF AMERICA

CONTENTS

TRANSLATORS' NOTE   vii

PREFACE   ix

INTRODUCTION   1

The Problem   1

Concepts and Definitions   2

    Affectivity • Cognitive vs Affective Behavior • Adaptation •
    Assimilation and Accommodation

Conclusion   5

AFFECTIVE VS COGNITIVE FUNCTION   6

Three Theories of Conduct   7

The Notion of Structure   9

STAGES OF INTELLECTUAL AND AFFECTIVE DEVELOPMENT   12

FIRST STAGE: HEREDITARY ORGANIZATIONS   16

An Inventory of Instincts   17

    Alimentary and Hunting Instincts • Instincts of Defense •
    Curiosity • Sexual Instincts • Parental Instincts • Social
    Instincts • Selfish Instincts • Play Instincts

Conclusion   19

SECOND STAGE: THE FIRST ACQUIRED FEELINGS   21

THIRD STAGE: AFFECTS REGULATING INTENTIONAL BEHAVIOR   26

Janet's Theory   26

    Theory   30

    ...s of Value and Interest   31

Affective Decentration and the Problem of "Object Choice"   36

Conclusion   42

FOURTH STAGE: INTUITIVE AFFECTS AND THE BEGINNING
OF INTERPERSONAL FEELINGS   44

Self-Estimation and Feelings of Superiority and Inferiority   47

The Beginning of Moral Feelings   49
   Obedience and Respect • Seminormative Feelings

FIFTH STAGE: NORMATIVE AFFECTS   59

The Problem of the Will   61

Will as Regulation of Regulations   63

Autonomous Feelings   65

SIXTH STAGE: IDEALISTIC FEELINGS AND FORMATION
OF THE PERSONALITY   69

GENERAL CONCLUSIONS   73

SUBJECT INDEX   75

TRANSLATORS' NOTE

The lectures in this volume were delivered at the Sorbonne during the 1953–1954 academic year. They represent Piaget's fullest statement not only on the nature of affectivity but also on the relation of affectivity to intelligence throughout development. They were first published in French in *Bulletin de Psychologie* (Paris), Vol. VII, No. 3-4, pp. 143–50, No. 6-7, pp. 346–61, No. 9-10, pp. 522–35, No. 12, pp. 699–701 (1954). Being lecture notes, they were presented in outline form. There were many headings, fragmentary statements, and inconsistencies of numbering, lettering, and tabulation. Since they in no way represented finished writing, the translators have extensively edited the original in order to ease the reader's burden. The outline form has been removed, fragments have been made into complete sentences, headings have been deleted or changed where necessary, and certain difficulties of Piaget's style and vocabulary have been omitted. In every case, changes were made to connect and clarify Piaget's ideas. It was never the translators' intention to add to or reinterpret what Piaget had written. If additions or reinterpretations exist, they represent failures to grasp or to express Piaget's meaning.

T. A. B.
C. E. K.

PREFACE

In this preface to the first English translation of Jean Piaget's most extensive discussion of affective development, I must begin by expressing my own feelings of sorrow and loss at his passing. Piaget died in Geneva, Switzerland, on September 16, 1980, a little more than a month after his eighty-fourth birthday. His monumental contribution to the psychology and philosophy of intellectual development can be seen in literally scores of books, monographs, and papers that describe an invariant sequence of stages from infancy to adulthood through which we come to understand the world and ourselves. No brief summary can document the richness of this legacy or its worldwide impact on developmental theorists and researchers; here I simply provide a context for his discussion of the relation between intelligence and affectivity.

Known primarily for his studies and theory of how children think and how they come to engage in adult-level scientific and philosophical thought, Piaget was also vitally interested in affective or emotional development. Early in his postdoctoral career he spent some time working in Bleuler's psychiatric clinic interviewing patients. Over the years he made many passing references to the affective side of intellectual functioning, and in several works he presented a detailed, stage-by-stage outline of both cognitive and affective characteristics of the developing child (*Play, Dreams and Imitation; Six Psychological Studies;* and, with Barbel Inhelder, *The Psychology of the Child*). As the present translators note, however, his major statement about the relation between intelligence and affectivity was made in a series of lectures delivered at the Sorbonne and published in 1954. Surprisingly, even after a steady stream of translations of his other writings began to appear in the 1960s, the text of those lectures was never translated into English. Some of us who were interested in this aspect of Piaget's theory passed around an incomplete and sketchy copy of an anonymous student's lecture notes, or searched in vain for the French journals in which the full text appeared. All of us, students old and new, are now indebted to T. A. Brown and C. E. Kaegi for the careful, clear, and felicitous translation presented in this monograph.

Issues in Theories of Affective Development

From the time of Plato until the Freudian impact on twentieth century personality theories, Western theorists tended to emphasize the rational, judgmental, information-processing, *cognitive* aspects of human nature.

The *affective* aspects were usually considered secondary and were discussed in attempts to answer four very different kinds of questions. 1. Even after we have explored the complex issues of how individuals come to understand the world, it is still possible to wonder why it is we bother to make the intellectual effort. Affect is often invoked as a causal mechanism that sets our cognitive apparatus in motion. This is the primary sense in which Piaget uses the term. 2. Once the individual becomes involved in a search for knowledge, we can ask how it is that he or she chooses to focus attention on one particular idea, object, or action rather than another. In addition to its energizing function, then, some see affect as having a primary role in determining the selection of specific goals. These first two conceptions deal with affect primarily in the sense of motivation. 3. Another view of affect arises in questions about subjective feelings of love, anger, depression, and the like that lead us to seek out or avoid specific people and experiences. 4. Finally, we can investigate the nature of the expressive aspect of affect —the smiles, shouts, or tears that often but not always let others know what we are feeling inside. Discussion of affect becomes confusing when these four aspects are not clearly delineated. Sometimes further confusion is introduced by circular reasoning, when we infer one aspect from another: "Why is he running away?" "Because he's afraid." "How do you know he's afraid?" "Because he's running away."

If it is assumed that cognition and affect are very separate functions, theorists must then provide some account of how they fit together. Looking at existing theories, Piaget noted several possible alternatives. Freud had created a developmental theory in which affect (an id function) was primary, acting as a source of cognitive activity (an ego function) and always playing a dominant role in determining the content of an individual's interests and concerns. By contrast, more philosophically oriented theorists tended to convey a picture of human beings whose cognitive function dominated actions, choices, and feelings. In this case, affect was more often seen as a fly in the ointment, interfering with the normal intellectual pursuits of rational men and women. Piaget noted a third alternative adopted by many contemporary learning theorists—a cognitive system operating according to principles of association, paired with an emotional-motivational system based on primary biological drives. These separate but equal systems are seen by learning theorists as interacting to determine whether an individual will learn or perform a given act, or choose a particular goal. All three of these alternative conceptions of the relation between emotion and intelligence were rejected by Piaget. He argued forcefully that affect and cognition were inseparable, that they constitute two different aspects of every sensorimotor or symbolic act.

Piaget's Approach

In the first two sections of this monograph, Piaget argues that affect is related to the *function* of intelligence—acting as an energizing force emerging from the disequilibration between assimilation and accommodation. Cognition provides the *structure* for this energy. Affect is likened to the gasoline that activates the car, while the engine provides structure for the energy and direction of the car's motion. Affect as "energetics" can combine with cognitive structural schemes to focus the individual's interest on a specific thing or idea. Because it influences an individual's choice of whether to exert intellectual effort, affect serves as a regulator of action. Because it influences the choice of specific goals, affect also plays a role in determining values (described here as internal interest projected outward so that things and people appear to have a certain worth). By regulating action and determining values, affect influences our tendency to approach or avoid situations; in turn, this influences the rate at which we develop knowledge, accelerating it in some areas, slowing it down or preventing it in others.

In the last long section of this monograph, Piaget outlines the developmental stages from birth through adolescence, showing parallels between characteristics of cognition and emotion-motivation at each level. For instance, stable feelings about specific people do not begin to arise until the fourth sensorimotor stage (at about six months of age) when the infant has constructed the scheme of the permanent object. This means, Piaget suggests, that there is necessarily a cognitive aspect of the infant's development of attachment. Later, in the preoperational stage beginning at about two years of age and extending over the next five years, the development of symbolic representation and language leads to the formation of stable concepts. The structural underpinning of these concepts also allows feelings to acquire stability over time. Still later, in the stage of concrete operations beginning at about seven years, the child's ability to construct classification hierarchies is accompanied by the emergence of a stable value hierarchy. This hierarchy represents the first emergence of what Piaget describes as the conservation of feelings. At the same time, we observe the beginning of a new level of moral judgment. Piaget believes that moral judgments are highly affective in nature. But for Piaget, moral judgments emerge from the general process of social cognitive development and not solely from the highly charged Oedipal conflict in which children's incestuous desires are repressed in the process of forming a superego, as Freud had argued.

Each of these examples illustrates Piaget's hypothesis that there are systematic shifts in the form as well as the content of affect as the child matures. He uses these and other examples to reinforce his argument that these shifts in affect are attributable to the structural properties underlying each new cognitive stage. By contrast with Freud's theory, in which the nature of both expressed and repressed affect remains relatively unchanged over time, Piaget's theory is one of the few truly developmental theories of emotion and motivation.

Rather than creating an artificial dichotomy between intelligence and affectivity, Piaget suggests that it may be more useful to make a distinction between transactions with physical objects and with people. Each domain has both cognitive and affective components; the meaning of an object always includes feelings and values, while feelings about people always involve interpretations and understandings.

Piaget's analysis of the social domain is further subdivided into parallel analyses of the child's conception of others and his or her conception of the self. He expected to find that the self-concept, and feelings about the self (self-esteem), would develop in the same way and at the same time as the child's understanding and feelings about physical objects and other people. Development in each one of these areas could act as a stimulant or a retardant for development in any other area. These expectations are just beginning to be tested in the recent resurgence of interest in social cognition.

While Piaget cites many different theorists in this monograph, he returns consistently to deal with Freud's hypotheses and findings. Sometimes Piaget's views can be used to supplement Freud's, as in Piaget's speculations about the importance of object permanence in the development of attachment. More often, the two theorists have very different views about the nature of cognition and affect in the child. Freud assumes that the mechanism of repression accounts for the fact that there are rarely any memories from the first year of life. Piaget believes that the very young infant has no symbolic function to allow him or her to *re-present* absent events. For Freud, feelings arising in the earliest interchanges with a caretaker are repressed but continue to dominate the child's or adult's feelings about other people (transference). This would imply that feelings are conserved over long periods of time during infancy and childhood. For Piaget, the similarity between earlier and later reactions is explained by the hypothesis that the child assimilates other persons to well-established social schemes: rules or patterns of interaction with people in authority, with peers, with family, and so on. The accompanying feelings are not simply retrieved from the past but are reconstructed to fit the individual's current interpersonal schemes. A child or adult may feel vulnerable because he or she interprets a situation as authority-related, not because another person evokes feelings about parents repressed from early childhood.

Piaget's contention that feelings may be reconstructed rather than retrieved as exact copies seems to be a forerunner of ideas that he later developed more fully in his general work on memory (*On Memory and Identity*; and, with Inhelder, *Memory and Intelligence*). In a set of interesting experiments he showed that memory does not recover faint copies of initial perceptions, but rather that the child reconstructs past events through a complex assimilative inferential process. Just as memories may change when the underlying cognitive structures change, feelings evoked in past situations may be altered by new and different ways of understanding the world.

If affect plays such a central role in human development, why did Piaget write so little about it? Why did he do so few empirical investigations of the topic? Piaget's central questions were concerned with *regularities* in human progress toward formal operations. Questions of affect arise for cognitive theorists only when they are concerned with *individual differences* in the rate of development or in the tendency to select a particular goal. Thus, Piaget was very concerned with explaining how children come to be capable of scientific and philosophical thought, but he was not at all interested in whether or how quickly a given child becomes a professional scientist or a philosopher.

Those of us concerned with issues of affective development itself, or its interaction with intellectual development, need not be bound by the limits of Piaget's interests. The theory as it is presented here does provide guidelines for investigating how children develop at different rates in different areas. It suggests new ways for psychologists and educators to look at issues of motivation—to explore, for example, the affective variables influencing the gap between what children are capable of understanding and what they actually choose to learn. And finally, as I have described elsewhere,[1] when the affective side of intelligence is considered along with the cognitive side, it becomes possible to develop new Piagetian approaches to the understanding of psychopathology—those instances when normal cognitive and affective development somehow goes awry.

Readers of this monograph should be aware that, while this integrated theory of affective development was new in these lectures, Piaget's discussion of his two-stage moral judgment theory is based on earlier work published in 1932 (*The Moral Judgment of the Child*). Those who are interested in a contemporary Piagetian cognitive developmental approach should familiarize themselves with current work by Kohlberg, Turiel, and others who are constructing a more detailed and differentiated view of stages and changes in moral and conventional judgment.

I should also emphasize that Piaget's theory of affect is still incomplete. Like other theorists, he chooses examples that fit best with his theory. Thus,

---

[1]P. A. Cowan, *Piaget: with Feeling* (New York: Holt, Rinehart & Winston, 1978).

as instances of affect in concrete and formal operational stages, he discusses 1. moral judgment, 2. value hierarchies, and 3. the function of *will* in choosing the less desired but more correct course of action. We will have to see whether other examples of personal and interpersonal feelings are consistent with his general model.

Finally, there is an omission in the current presentation that provides us all with an exciting opportunity. Though decades have passed since Piaget suggested that cognition and affect are actually "two sides of the same coin," there has been almost no empirical work that tests whether they do show similar formal characteristics when we examine them in a given child or adult. In almost every section of the present work, there are ideas ripe for systematic exploration. Perhaps the publication of this monograph will stimulate this challenging and much-needed line of research.

PHILIP A. COWAN
Department of Psychology
University of California, Berkeley

INTRODUCTION

The theme of these lectures was suggested by discussions that took place during the course last year. In those discussions, it was claimed that our study of intellectual development lapsed into intellectualism because it arbitrarily isolated intelligence and neglected the relationship between intellectual and affective life. The purpose of this year's course is, therefore, to study this relationship.

The Problem

Today no one would think of denying that there is constant interaction between affectivity and intelligence. To say that they are indissociable can mean two very different things, however. In one sense, it could mean that affectivity speeds up or slows down intellectual functioning without modifying the structures of intelligence as such. This stimulating or hindering role is incontestable. Students who are eager to learn have more enthusiasm for studying and learn more easily. Conversely, more than half of those students who are weak in mathematics probably owe their weakness to an affective block. Most of them feel they have a particular inferiority in this subject. The fact that such blocks may temporarily hinder a student's understanding or retention of the rules of addition does not, however, alter the rules in any way.

In the second sense, the indissociability of intelligence and affectivity could mean that affectivity changes intellectual structures and is, therefore, the source of new knowledge or new cognitive operations. Several authors have held this point of view. Wallon, for instance, emphasized that emotion, far from playing an inhibitory role in every case, sometimes plays the role of an excitant. He believed this was particularly true on the sensorimotor level where it is known that enjoyment causes developmental progress. Preyer's infant, for example, lifted and dropped his blanket 119 successive times. Obviously, he was motivated to do this by enjoyment of what he was

1

doing. From Wallon's position to the belief that affectivity is the source of knowledge is a small step, however, and it is a step that some disciples of Wallon have taken. Philippe Malrieu, for instance, held that affectivity was a positive determinant of intellectual progress, particularly on the sensorimotor level. For him, affectivity was the source of structuration (*Les émotions et la personnalité de l'enfant,* Vrin, 1952). Ribot also subscribed to this idea. In his classic *Logique des sentiments,* he contended that feeling disturbed logical reasoning and could create new structures like those seen in legal pleading. Such pleas constituted, according to Ribot, a special affective logic; but he demonstrated little except the paralogisms to which affectivity leads. Passion uses logic to its advantage by making deductions from shaky premises, but it does not create new reasoning structures. A similar criticism might be applied to C. Perelman's revival of the notion of *rhetoric* to designate the sorts of informal methods used to generate conviction in others. While it is true that rhetoric is partly inspired by affectivity, that does not mean affectivity creates new structures.

Concepts and Definitions

In order to choose between these alternatives, the problem of the relationship between affectivity and intelligence will be studied genetically. We shall begin by recalling several guiding definitions.

AFFECTIVITY   The term, affectivity includes feelings, properly so-called, as well as the various drives or tendencies (*tendances*) including "higher tendencies" such as the will. Some authors, it is true, distinguish between affective factors such as emotions or feelings and conative factors such as drives or will. We shall not do so, however, because the difference between the affective and the conative appears to be only a matter of degree. This may be illustrated by considering Pierre Janet's definition of feelings. He based his definition on the economy of behavior[1] and defined feelings as regulations of the force an individual has at his disposal. From the same point of view, the will would only be a regulation of the elementary regulations constituted by feelings.

COGNITIVE VS AFFECTIVE BEHAVIOR   It is impossible to find behavior arising from affectivity alone without any cognitive elements. It is equally impossible to find behavior composed only of cognitive elements. Nevertheless, cognitive functions, from perception and sensorimotor schemes up to

---

[1]Piaget takes care to distinguish between "conduct" and "behavior," conduct being behavior including consciousness. Since conduct sounds unnatural in English, behavior will be used. It should be understood, however, that it does not imply behavior in the behaviorist sense.— Translators

abstract intelligence with formal operations, will be distinguished from affective functions. This seems necessary because, although cognitive and affective factors are indissociable in an individual's concrete behavior, they appear to be different in nature. The following considerations make this clear.

Regarding the assertion that there is no cognitive mechanism without affective elements, it is obvious that affective factors are involved even in the most abstract forms of intelligence. For a student to solve an algebra problem or a mathematician to discover a theorem, there must be intrinsic interest, extrinsic interest, or a need at the beginning. While working, states of pleasure, disappointment, eagerness, as well as feelings of fatigue, effort, boredom, etc, come into play. At the end of the work, feelings of success or failure may occur; and finally, the student may experience aesthetic feelings stemming from the coherence of his solution. In ordinary acts of practical intelligence, the lack of dissociation between cognitive and affective mechanisms is more evident still. Intrinsic or extrinsic interest is always evident. Perceptual activity, too, involves affective factors such as perceptual choice, pleasant or unpleasant feelings, the affective tonality of indifference, and aesthetic feelings.

Regarding the opposite situation, it is also obvious that there is no such thing as a purely affective state devoid of cognitive elements. Konrad Lorenz, studying the instincts of birds, established the existence of very precisely determined perceptual configurations that are innate and specific. He called these Innate Releasing Mechanisms. In ducklings, for example, certain movements peculiar to the mother's gait release the drive to follow her. Another illustration would be the sexual instinct of certain species of parrots. In these species, the sexual behavior of the male is triggered by perception of light blue color. Instincts are not, therefore, set off by affective factors alone; their release also requires specific perceptual stimulations. By artificially reproducing these stimulations, Lorenz was easily able to deceive animals. Inversely, the slightest modification of perceptual configurations can prevent release of drives.

Emotion, too, involves perceptual discriminations. For example, Wallon has demonstrated that fear in infants is originally linked to a proprioceptive sensation of loss of balance. It is also known that fear of darkness in infancy and conditioned fears of every sort occur in response to perceptual stimulations. Cognitive factors play a role, therefore, in elementary feelings and are even more apparent in complex feelings where intellectual elements are increasingly included.

ADAPTATION It might be said, nevertheless, that purely cognitive or purely affective factors can be found in the most general characteristics of behavior such as adaptation, assimilation, accommodation, and equilibration. All behavior is adaptation and all adaptation is the establishment of equilibrium between the organism and its environment. We act only if we are momentarily disequilibrated. Claparède demonstrated that such disequilibria are felt as awareness of the unique affective impression, need. He further demonstrated that behavior stops when need is satisfied and that this return to equilibrium is indicated by a feeling of satisfaction. Obviously, Claparède's schema[2] is very general. There is no nutrition without alimentary need, no work without need, nor any intellectual act without a question or without a gap being felt and, therefore, without disequilibrium or need. If all of this indicates that there is an affective dimension to the general characteristics of behavior, the fact remains that the notions of equilibrium and disequilibrium have fundamental significance from the intellectual as well as from the affective point of view. Gestalt theory, for example, defines perception as an equilibration; the law of good form is a law of equilibrium; and in my own theory, intellectual operations tend towards forms of equilibrium (cf reversibility).

ASSIMILATION AND ACCOMMODATION   If adaptation is examined from the point of view of assimilation and accommodation, this same lack of dissociation between cognitive and affective factors is apparent. Assimilation is that aspect of adaptation which conserves form or organization. Accommodation is that aspect which modifies form as a function of the external situation. Both notions apply to forms of behavior and thought as well as to organic structures.

In psychological assimilation viewed from the cognitive perspective, objects are incorporated into forms or schemes of behavior. Assimilation may, therefore, be perceptual, sensorimotor, or conceptual. In perceptual assimilation, objects are perceived relative to existing perceptual schemes. In sensorimotor assimilation, they are incorporated into schemes of motor action as, for instance, when a one year old child pulls on his blanket in order to obtain some object sitting on it out of reach. In such an act, the baby uses his blanket as an intermediary and assimilates it into prehensile schemes that have already been constructed. Finally, conceptual assimilations are those where a new object is conceived or understood because it is incorporated into forms or structures of internal action or thought. In other

[2]In the "Author's Preface" to *The Mechanisms of Perception,* Piaget distinguishes his use of the words *schème* and *schéma* in the following way: the first is operative in the sense of an instrument of generalization, the second is figurative in the sense of an image or topographical sketch. In order to preserve this distinction, the cognates of these terms will be used.— Translators

words, they are assimilations into the systems of mental operations that the subject has constructed.

The cognitive aspect of psychological accommodation is seen if the object resists assimilation into any existing scheme. In that case, the schemes are not adapted to the new object and must be modified. When the object does not resist too much to be assimilable but still resists enough to cause accommodation, adaptation occurs. Adaptation is, therefore, an equilibrium between accommodation and assimilation.

If assimilation and accommodation have their cognitive side, as is indicated by what has just been said, they, like all other characteristics of behavior, have an affective side as well. The affective aspect of assimilation is interest, defined by Dewey as assimilation to the self; the cognitive aspect is understanding. Accommodation in its affective aspect is interest in the object in as much as it is new. In its cognitive aspect, accommodation is the adjustment of schemes of thought to phenomena.

Conclusion

In summary, affective states that have no cognitive elements are never seen, nor are behaviors found that are wholly cognitive. This brings up the question of just what the relationship of intelligence to affectivity is. Does affectivity create new structures on the intellectual plane and, reciprocally, does intelligence create new feelings? Or is the relationship between intelligence and affectivity only functional? In the latter case, affectivity would play the role of an energy source on which the functioning but not the structures of intelligence would depend. It would be like gasoline, which activates the motor of an automobile but does not modify its structure. This second thesis is the one we defend throughout this discussion.

AFFECTIVE VS COGNITIVE FUNCTION

We propose to show that even if affectivity can cause behavior, even if it is constantly involved in the functioning of intelligence, and even if it can speed up or slow down intellectual development, it nevertheless does not, itself, generate structures of behavior and does not modify the structures in whose functioning it intervenes. In order to clarify this idea, let us review some examples.

First let us take the case of mathematical operations. Feelings of success or failure may facilitate or inhibit a student's learning math, but the structure of mathematical operations will not be changed. A child may make mistakes because of affective interference; but even so, he will not invent new rules of addition. One child may understand more quickly than another, but the operation will always be the same.

A second example might be taken from logic. Consider, for instance, the seriation of five weights in the Binet-Simon test. At issue is a logical operation implying transitivity. If A is lighter than B and if B is lighter than C, then it follows *necessarily* that A is lighter than C. This operation is normally performed around six and a half or seven years. If the child is encouraged, the results may be better; if not, there may be regression to the level of preoperational thought. In either case, no new structure will be seen. The operation is successful or not; that is all. From time to time, authors have taken regressions to previous stages of thought to be new structures. As mentioned earlier, Ribot considered one form of such regressions, i.e. the paralogisms seen in impassioned argument, to constitute novel forms of reason. As also mentioned, we do not agree.

A third and final example might be perception. It is quite evident that affectivity constantly influences perceptual activity. Different subjects will not perceive the same elements of a complex figure, their choices being inspired by different interests; nor will children and adults perceive the same details. Nevertheless, the laws that constitute the structure of perception remain the same in all cases.

In order to see this better, let us examine an experiment that concluded otherwise. Bruner studied illusions of over-estimation by having subjects compare the diameter of a metal disc with that of a silver dollar. When the diameters were equal, the size of the dollar was over-estimated. Bruner said that this was due to the interest people have in dollars. The fact that the magnitude of the over-estimation varied according to the individual, Bruner believed, occurred because over-estimation is proportional to the intensity of a person's interest. Examining the facts more closely, it seems questionable to say that interest is the direct cause of this perceptual over-estimation. Two hypotheses are possible. Either interest directly generates the illusion, or interest is only an indirect cause.

Bearing on this are my own and Lambercier's experiments on the estimation of the length of a rod in comparison to a standard. These studies establish a systematic illusion called "over-estimation of measuring." The standard rod is over-estimated when it is used as a standard of comparison, but if the order of comparison is inverted by switching the standard and the rod to be measured without the subject seeing the switch, the illusion is reversed. It seems likely, therefore, that interest in the dollar leads to perceptual *centration,* thereby causing the subject to take the dollar as the standard of comparison and fall victim to the measuring illusion. In that case, Bruner's illusion would be only functional.

We can extract a provisional conclusion from such facts and state the themes we shall develop. The first of these is that although affectivity is constantly at work in the functioning of thought, it does not create new structures of reasoning. This means that affectivity does not create laws of equilibrium which are more and more differentiated from their content and independent of functioning. The second of our provisional conclusions is that the energetics of behavior arise from affectivity whereas the structures arise from cognitive functions. This distinction of structure and energetics demonstrates clearly that even though intelligence and affectivity are not separable in concrete conduct, they are different in nature.

Several authors have supported related points of view and have also distinguished energetic and structural aspects of behavior. Let us examine three of these now classical theories in order to delineate our own.

Three Theories of Conduct

Claparède attributed a very important role in the workings of intelligence to *interest.* According to his theory, all behavior implied a goal or finality, i.e. a more or less conscious intention, which was always defined by affectivity in the form of interest. He contended, moreover, that all behavior presupposed a *"technique"* (method of accomplishing a desired aim) consisting of a group of means used to attain the goal. The technique, according to Claparède, was determined, by cognitive functions such as perception or intelligence.

Such a sketchy two-part division does not appear satisfactory to us. In the first place, goals presuppose an interaction of affectivity and intelligence. Even if interest is the source of motivation, it is not sufficient to define goals in the sense intended by Claparède. A goal depends on the entire field and will change according to the intellectual means that the subject has available. Goals, therefore, include cognitive elements. In the second place, means are not purely cognitive as Claparède said they were. The technique by which a goal is attained requires coordinations, regulations, and always presupposes an energy whose origin appears to be essentially affective. Persistence during the course of an act illustrates this point. It seems, therefore, that the problem we have set ourselves and the distinction we believe it is necessary to make arise both with respect to means and with respect to goals.

Pierre Janet's is another theory of this sort. According to Janet, all behavior involves two types of "action." First, there is a *primary action*, defined as the relationship between the subject and external objects in the form of things or people on which the subject acts. Action originates from structures of different levels such as reflexes, perceptions, and the like, which are always cognitive. The second sort of action, called by Janet the *secondary action*, consists of the subject's reaction to his own action. It includes all of the regulations that reinforce or brake the primary action. Examples of this are the sense of effort, the feeling of fatigue anticipating failure, or termination reactions such as enjoyment or letdown which are felt when an action is completed. The secondary action is, therefore, a regulation of forces that control the internal economy of action and constitute its energetics. For Janet, secondary action arises from affectivity alone.

This distinction, which seems to overlap the one we have proposed, presents an equivocation analogous to Claparède's and, like his theory, appears inadequate. Again, this is because affectivity plays a role even in the primary action. For example, affectivity is involved in choosing which object is to be perceived within the total field. Because of this, the relationship of the subject to the object must include an energetics and must involve affectivity. Conversely, the system of secondary regulation consists of two sorts of controls, i.e. internal regulations and regulations of exchanges with the environment. The latter are not just a matter of energetics since they require cognitive elements or structures. Structure and energetics or affective and cognitive elements are, therefore, simultaneously present in primary as well as secondary actions.

Kurt Lewin provides a final example of a theory where structure and energetics are distinguished. Lewin, a student of Köhler, applies the theory of form to problems of affectivity and social psychology. In doing so, he considerably broadens the concepts used in gestalt theory. Besides the notion of the perceptual field, he invokes the notion of the *total field* which embraces the self and is, itself, structured in a certain way. Structure is involved, therefore, not only in perception of the object but also in the relationship of the subject to that object. The "solicitous nature" of the object, which Lewin speaks of, results from the configuration of the total field. In other words, it brings structural properties of the object and inclinations of the subject together. Lewin makes the structure of the total field the object of his topological psychology and divides it into two inseparable but different aspects. One aspect is the *structure* of the field. This is perceptual or intellectual and, therefore, cognitive. The other aspect is the field's *dynamics* and is affective.

This division is obviously very similar to the one we are proposing. We prefer the term energetics to the term dynamics because the latter stands in opposition to "static." If dynamics is used, people might think that we ascribe a dynamic quality to affectivity and a static quality to intelligence, which is incorrect. The structure-energetics opposition seems less ambiguous.

The Notion of Structure

First, let us examine whether it is legitimate to reserve, as we shall do, the term structure for the cognitive functions. People often speak of "affective structures," but this expression can have two meanings. The first meaning is a metaphorical one which is of no concern here. The second is a stricter and more profound meaning related to the fact that certain affective systems end up as structures. This would be the case, for example, when interests are projected onto objects in the form of values. In certain cases, these may be arranged into "scales of values" resembling seriation structures. Moral and social feelings would be even better examples of affects that crystallize into well-determined structures. Far from contradicting our thesis, however, the existence of structures such as these confirms it. This is because affective structures are isomorphic with intellectual structures and, in fact, result from intellectualization. Such intellectualization exists from the moment feelings are structured. Only energetics remain purely affective. The ambiguity as to whether structures are cognitive or affective stems, at least in part, from the fact that structure and functioning or intelligence and affectivity are indissociable in all behavior. The ambiguity comes from the difficulty of separating the cognitive and affective elements which closely interpenetrate in the most varied situations.

A further source of confusion is the fact that it is easier to recognize a structure than to give a general definition of it. One might, for example, attempt to characterize structure by various oppositions and begin by contrasting *structure* with *energetics*. Unlike energetics, structure is defined without making an appeal to strength or weakness or to more or less. In gestalt theory, when some structure is said to be "more pregnant"[3] than another, it is obviously a question of two qualitatively different structures and not of two structures of different intensity. In contrast to this, a feeling can be stronger or weaker. *Structure versus function* would be a second opposition that might be considered. Here structure results from functioning while functioning implies preexisting structures (cf the distinction between organic structures and functions in physiology). Finally, the opposition between *structure* and *content* might be examined. This is a problem analogous to the form-matter opposition. Even though the theoretical opposition in this instance is very clear, it is often impossible to distinguish these two factors in the course of development because structures are only progressively differentiated from content. On the level of preoperational intelligence, structures are not very well equilibrated and can hardly be separated from the content of action at all. On the level of concrete operations, the child is capable of carrying out certain operations in practice, e.g. seriations. This implies structure, but the child does not recognize this structure and will be incapable of reproducing the operation he has just carried out successfully in one situation in an analogous but nonidentical situation. Only at the age of formal thought, beginning around 12 years, are structures well-differentiated and transfers of this kind possible. Let us recall in this regard that if affectivity cannot modify structures, it still constantly influences their contents. For example, it is interest and, therefore, affectivity that makes the child decide to seriate objects and decide which objects to seriate. Affectivity also will decide the activity and content of classification operations. In so far as the structure of operations is not distinct from their content, the two may often be confused; but in neither case will affectivity change the rules of seriation or classification.

If, alternatively, one wishes to give a positive definition of structure, the most important characteristic is *closure*. A structure is a closed totality. The series of whole numbers, for example, may be generated by repeating simple operations, such as addition, multiplication, etc, that form a closed system. These operations constitute a structure.

---

[3] *Prégnance* is a technical term taken from Gestalt psychology. "The principle of *Praegnanz*, first formulated by Wertheimer with reference to perception, asserts that the organization of the field tends to be as simple and clear as the given conditions allow." Editor's note in *Productive Thinking* by M. Wertheimer (New York: Harper & Brothers, 1959), p. 239—Translators

Let us make clear, however, that closure does not mean completion. One structure can always be replaced by another structure. One system can always be integrated into a more general system constructed later. This was the case when the system of whole numbers was integrated into the system of fractions or into the systems of rational, irrational, and complex numbers. The closure of a structure designates, therefore, a completeness or stability which is at least provisional but which may be toppled at some later time as the system moves toward a broader and more stable equilibrium. In contrast to this, energetics are always open.

Finally, we should remark that cognitive systems are more or less structured and are, therefore, more or less closed depending on their level of development. Because of this, they are more or less profoundly penetrated by affectivity according to the level under consideration.

STAGES OF INTELLECTUAL AND AFFECTIVE DEVELOPMENT

We propose to look at the relationship between intelligence and affectivity from the genetic point of view. If our previous hypotheses are correct, we shall be able to put intellectual structures and the levels of affective development in parallel, stage by stage. Since structure does not exist without energetics and, reciprocally, since every new structure involves a new form of energetic regulation, a particular sort of cognitive structure will be found in concert with every new type of affective regulation. Before proposing a general outline of these parallels, however, let us examine two possible objections against putting cognitive structures and affective regulations into correspondence.

To begin with, it might be objected that there are no immediate givens of a cognitive nature although there appear to be givens of this sort that are affective. All ideas, the argument continues, are constructed; all knowledge implies assimilation or interpretation. Immediate reading of experience is not possible since a system of reference is always necessary. For instance, to establish whether or not a line is vertical requires that it be put into correspondence with a system of coordinates. Similarly, simultaneity is not something that is verified intuitively. Judgments of simultaneity are made by using spatio-temporal systems of synchronization, and this takes time. In contrast to this, emotions and feelings seem to be immediate givens that are independent of all intentional construction.

We respond to this objection that it is, in fact, only a romantic prejudice that makes us suppose that affective phenomena constitute immediate givens or innate and ready-made feelings similar to Rousseau's "conscience." In truth, there is as much construction in the affective domain as there is in the cognitive. Even literary psychology has stressed this fact. Stendhal, for example, did so in his theory of crystallization, and Proust did so by utilizing the relativity of feelings (cf the successive visions of M. de Charlus)

12

to construct his characters. In effect, Proust created the reality of his characters' personalities by coordinating their subjective points of view.

Psychoanalysis, too, has taken as its task to demonstrate how feelings are constructed. It holds that what a person feels at any given moment is dependent upon his entire history. If Freud and his followers oversimplified this construction by positing an affective drive at the start and defining all affects in terms of metamorphoses of libido as it is transferred from one object to another, they were, nevertheless, correct to stress the genesis and construction of affective realities. A complex in the psychoanalytic sense is a scheme elaborated in the course of an individual's history. It evolves through constant transformation and repeated application to diverse and ceaselessly recurring situations. Its construction is analogous to the progressive construction of a system of concepts and relations. This indicates quite clearly that there is a schematization of feelings just as there are schemes of intelligence.

A second objection that is often raised has to do with the fact that intelligence involves operations and that these give rise to notions of conservation. If that is so, parallelism between intelligence and affectivity would require that analogues of conservation and operations be found in the affective domain. Many people contend, however, that feelings are not conserved and that there is, therefore, no evidence that affective operations exist.

Our response is that certainly there are elementary feelings, such as interpersonal likes and dislikes, that are not conserved, but that these constitute what we shall call "nonnormative" feelings. They are comparable to preoperational representations and not to invariant operational ones. At the higher levels of affective function like the level of autonomous morality, we shall find, in addition to nonnormative feelings of this sort, a whole system of normative feelings, e.g. the feeling of duty, which assures the conservation of certain values. The difference between a nonnormative feeling and a normative feeling is the same as the difference between a spontaneous feeling like gratitude and the same feeling integrated into a normative system. Moral feelings constitute, in fact, a veritable logic of feelings, albeit in a sense very different from that in which Ribot employed this expression. Morality is, therefore, a logic of action in the same way that logic is a morality of thought.

If normative feelings constitute the affective analogue of intellectual conservation, they give no inkling as to the "affective operations" that make this conservation possible. These, we believe, will be found in the system of the will. As William James demonstrated, the will comes into play only when it is necessary to choose between two drives or tendencies. It involves, therefore, a regulation of regulations comparable to an operation. We shall

Table 1 Stages of intellectual and affective development

A. Sensorimotor intelligence	Intra-individual feelings
I. *Hereditary organizations*	*Hereditary organizations*
These include reflexes and instincts present at birth.	These include instinctual drives and all other inborn affective reactions.
II. *First acquired schemes*	*First acquired feelings*
These include the first habits and differentiated perceptions. They appear before the sensorimotor intelligence, properly so-called.	These are joys, sorrows, pleasantness, and unpleasantness linked to perceptions as well as differentiated feelings of contentment and disappointment linked to action.
III. *Sensorimotor intelligence*	*Affects regulating intentional behavior*
This includes the structures acquired from six or eight months up to the acquisition of language in the second year.	These regulations, intended in Janet's sense, include feelings linked to the activation and retardation of action along with termination reactions such as feelings of success or failure.
B. Verbal intelligence	Interpersonal feelings
IV. *Preoperational representations*	*Intuitive affects*
Here action begins to be internalized. Although this allows thought, such thought is not yet reversible.	These include elementary interpersonal feelings and the beginnings of moral feelings.
V. *Concrete operations*	*Normative affects*
This stage lasts from approximately 7 or 8 until 10 or 11 years of age. It is marked by the acquisition of elementary operations of classes and relations. Formal thought is still not possible.	This stage is characterized by the appearance of autonomous moral feelings with intervention of the will. What is just and what is unjust no longer depend on obedience to a rule.
VI. *Formal operations*	*Idealistic feelings*
This stage begins around 11 or 12 years, but it is not completely realized until 14 or 15. It is characterized by thought employing the logic of propositions freed from their content.	In this stage feelings for other people are overlaid by feelings for collective ideals. Parallel to this is the elaboration of the personality where the individual assigns himself a role and goals in social life.

see later on that if the notion of reversibility is introduced there is no longer any need to suppose, as James did, that the will involves the mysterious appearance of some "additional force."

In conclusion, then, let us not be surprised if the comparison between affective states and acts of intelligence cannot be pushed too far; and since we specifically deny that affectivity can create new structures, let us not be surprised if feelings do not yield notions identical to the invariants of intelligence. But neither let us go on to radically oppose feelings and intellectual structures. Feelings, without being structures by themselves, are structurally organized by being intellectualized. When someone claims to have demonstrated a fundamental heterogeneity of affective and intellectual life, he ordinarily has made the error of comparing feelings on one level to intellectual operations on a different level. If care is taken to compare cognitive structures and affective systems that are *contemporary* in development, however, it becomes possible to speak of a term-by-term correspondence such as the one summarized in Table 1.

This table indicates the plan of exposition we shall follow. Two periods are distinguished, one before and one after language is acquired. These correspond to nonsocialized and socialized behavior. Intra-individual feelings are those that accompany the subject's action whatever it may be, whereas interpersonal feelings have to do with affective exchanges between people. Each period is composed of three successive stages.[4]

---

[4]It should be noted that the numbering of these stages does *not* correspond to Piaget's usual numbering of the substages of the sensorimotor intelligence. Here, Stage II includes the second and third sensorimotor substages described elsewhere by Piaget, and Stage III includes the fourth, fifth, and sixth sensorimotor substages.—Translators

FIRST STAGE: HEREDITARY ORGANIZATIONS

Let us review and discuss several classical points of view in order to specify certain definitions and dispel some ambiguities of language. As Table 1 indicates, the first stage is one of reflexes and instincts. We, therefore, focus first on the nature of the elementary drives[5] which immediately leads to the ambiguity of the term *instinct*. This is our initial topic for discussion.

Instinct, in fact, designates both a technique and a drive. The *technique* (in German, *instinkt*) is a *structure* composed of reflexes coordinated into a single system which permits satisfaction of a need. An example would be the coordinated reflexes of sucking and swallowing which satisfy alimentary needs. The *drive* (in French, *tendance;* in German, *trieb*) is the hereditary need itself and corresponds to the *energetic* element of an instinct. Every instinctive technique presupposes a drive that it will satisfy. Ambiguity has arisen because some people think of instincts as only being drives, while others have accepted, alongside instincts which include inherited techniques, instincts without technique. Claparède, for example, thought that the instinct of imitation could be reduced to an "instinct to conform," and that the technique of this instinct was not inborn but was learned as Guillaume, among others, had shown.

In fact, it is difficult to isolate and enumerate instinctive drives for two reasons. The first is that innate does not mean contemporaneous with birth. Certain drives like the sexual drives are activated by maturation. It is very difficult, therefore, to decide what comes from biological maturation and what comes from social learning. This fact leads to the second reason that the distinction is so difficult, i.e. all developmental levels are influenced by the environment (cf Verlaine's experiment on the nest-building of female canaries). Consider, for example, the alleged instinctive fears of small chil-

---

[5]In the lectures from which this book is taken, Piaget included emotions as a form of hereditary affective organization. During preparation of the translation, he requested that the section on emotions be omitted. "That part of my lectures is completely out of date and no longer has any value." His wishes have been respected.—Translators

16

dren such as fear of the dark or the fear of reptiles. Watson made a game of conditioning and deconditioning these fears at will. William James related that his son at 18 months of age was afraid of a frog which, when he was eight months old, he had found amusing. Must we believe that this was a case of instinctive fear with late maturation? Is it not more likely that a child can conceive of a larger number of pleasant or unpleasant possibilities when he is 18 months of age than he could at eight months? Changes in behavior may be evidence of intellectual development, but affective development may be involved as well. Perhaps the frog became the object of a transference or took on symbolic meaning, etc. In a general way then, let us recognize that every drive is inserted into a context that goes far beyond it and that this context includes both intellectual and acquired elements.

An Inventory of Instincts

The second focus of these remarks will have to do with the many attempts to inventory or enumerate instincts. Watson, for instance, distinguished three unconditioned primitive emotions, i.e. fear, anger, and affection. K. M. B. Bridges enumerated twenty instinctive drives appearing between birth and two years. Rather than examining all of these, we shall limit ourselves to the inventory proposed by Larguier des Bancels in "L'instinct et l'émotion" (see Dumas' *Nouveau traité*). Des Bancels' list was based on the works of William James, McDougall, and Thorndike. It distinguished eight instincts.

ALIMENTARY AND HUNTING INSTINCTS   There is no problem as far as the alimentary instincts, themselves, are concerned. They involve a biological need, differentiated organs, and an hereditary organization of reflexes designed to satisfy the need. In some animals, however, hunting behavior is due in large part to acquisition. For example, Kuo found that the predatory instinct in cats is quite weak when they are raised away from the mother. Hunting in these animals owes a great deal to learning and imitation. With regard to children, traces of the hunting instinct are too faint for us to be able to speak of it with certitude despite the declarations of Stanley Hall.

INSTINCTS OF DEFENSE   The so-called defensive instincts are composed of primary instincts such as behaviors that defend the organism against toxins and other inborn aversive reactions as well as derived behaviors in the form of fears and aggressions. In as much as it is a question of inhibition, even of aversion, one can rightly suppose a reflex mechanism. For fear and aggression, the label is less certain. Adler and Pierre Bovet, approaching the problem along different biases, studied instincts of domination and combat.

They found a relationship between aggressiveness and fear. We question, however, whether the fact that young boys fight justifies speaking of a combative instinct. There are neither differentiated organs nor hereditary organizations of reflexes for this behavior. At most, one could speak of a drive without a technique. It seems more likely that aggression or the "drive to assert oneself" results from interactions between individuals and, therefore, from social learning rather than from an hereditary aggressive need.

CURIOSITY   A need to know manifests itself very early as, for example, in the circular reactions[6] of the infant. To speak of this as instinct, however, is only to say that cognitive functions are innate. The term curiosity qualifies a group of behaviors more than it characterizes them. For this reason, calling curiosity innate seems to us only to advance the truism that cognitive activity responds to hereditary needs. In other words, since curiosity conveys the general idea of the functioning of various organs (which is the source of intelligence) rather than the functioning of some particular organ, there is no reason to make a special instinct of it.

SEXUAL INSTINCTS   Sexual behavior certainly involves instincts since it is a specialized behavior with its own goals and special organs.

PARENTAL INSTINCTS   People often speak of either a maternal or a paternal instinct. In either case, the legitimacy of the term instinct is doubtful. Perhaps among animals there is a connection between endocrine mechanisms and maternal behavior, but in humans the existence of such an instinct is questionable. The classical proof invoked is the little girl's play with dolls. What part does imitation play, however, or projection, or, above all, symbolization used to relive scenes experienced within the family? The child reproached for not finishing her soup will reproduce the incident with her doll. Either she will scold the doll, and often with more severity than her parents did her; or she will give her parents a lesson by treating her doll with more psychological understanding than they used with her. In both cases, she will find a resolution of the conflict. The part maternal instinct, if it exists, plays in such behavior is quite weak in relation to other components. More generally, maternal and paternal behavior can be considered

[6]Piaget distinguishes three types of circular reactions during the sensorimotor period. The first two types, called primary and secondary, are seen during the stage called "first acquired schemes" in this text. The third type, labeled tertiary, appears during what is here called the stage of "sensorimotor intelligence." All have to do with the active reproduction of interesting results produced by action although the tertiary circular reaction goes beyond simple repetition to vary the result sought in different ways. While all circular reactions may be said to manifest curiosity, none is instinctual or inborn.—Translators

less as evidence of an instinct than as an extension of affectivity at every level.

SOCIAL INSTINCTS   The idea of social instincts lends itself to the same criticism. Man's social behavior is less the result of hereditary transmission than of an individual's interactions with others. Just as is the case in language acquisition, social experience plays a powerful role. At most one might speak of a social drive without any inborn technique, but social behavior seems to be explained better in terms of social interactions than in terms of instincts. To illustrate this point, let us consider Charlotte Bühler's work. Bühler observed that children's first smiles are addressed to people, and this has often been invoked as proof of a differentiated hereditary sociability. In fact, however, smiles are rapidly generalized to all sorts of objects. What differentiates other people from objects for the young child is movement. That being so, there is some question as to whether a smile specific to people really exists. It seems equally probable that the child's smile is, at first, a reaction to anything that moves. If that were so, the smile of a three-month old would differ from that of a five-week old in nature, not degree. We shall limit ourselves here to posing the question and to recognizing that the label instinct is in this case quite uncertain.

SELFISH INSTINCTS   Selfish instincts, or what might also be called instincts of self-preservation, are also included in des Bancels' list. As with curiosity, and this time unquestionably, we are dealing with the sort of expression that is tautological or devoid of meaning. These alleged instincts are only the tendency of a living being to perservere in its functioning. Far from designating specialized behaviors, they cover the totality of the organism and its functions. To speak of instincts of self-preservation is to say that the living being is living.

PLAY INSTINCTS   The same remark applies to the so-called play instincts. Certainly all children play and do so spontaneously. If we see play as a form of pre-exercise, as Karl Groos thought we should, we can speak of instinctive drives corresponding to future adult activities. If, as in the current fashion, we call play the typical activity of the child incapable of conduct of a higher level (Buytendijk), then to speak of a play instinct is to say that the child has an instinct to be a child. Again, we have only a tautology.

Conclusion

Our purpose is not to resolve the problems of instinct. For the most part, we leave unanswered the questions we have raised. From the preceding discussion let us keep in mind that the term instinct is used in three very different ways. We can distinguish three cases. The first is where the term instinct designates a specific drive, well-defined behaviors in the form of hereditary sensorimotor structures, and differentiated organs. Nutritive and sexual instincts would be examples. The second case is where the term loses all meaning and only designates one or every aspect of the organism's activity. Curiosity and play would be included here. The third and final definition is where ambiguity remains. In this case, the name "instinct" is given to some affective constant, to some need or specialized feeling, which may include an hereditary element but which can also be explained by interactions within the individual or by interactions of the individual with other people.

At least one remark remains valid in every case: from whatever level one views it, every drive is integrated into a context that goes beyond it. Every instinct, even the most incontestably hereditary, is manifested in complex behaviors where the most diverse and alien elements intermingle; *and these integrated wholes undergo transformations.* Whether these transformations result from drives being transferred from one object to another, as Freudianism claims, or whether they arise from incessant reconstruction remains to be determined. We shall, however, leave that question until our discussion of the third developmental stage.

SECOND STAGE: THE FIRST
ACQUIRED FEELINGS

Let us begin our discussion of the second stage by considering its characteristics from the cognitive point of view. The first acquired behaviors are
found in this stage. These take the form of reflexes that have been differentiated as a function of experience. There are two aspects to this. There is
a passive aspect which involves conditionings, and there is an active aspect
which involves circular reactions where the infant actively repeats results
obtained by chance. Among the latter, it is possible to distinguish both
primary circular reactions, defined as those involving the subject's body
only, and secondary circular reactions in which external objects play a role.
All such acquisitions indicate a progressive differentiation of perceptions as
a function of objects and situations.

If we shift to the affective point of view, we again find that two developments take place. To begin with, *perceptual affects* make their appearance.
These are feelings such as pleasure, pain, pleasantness, unpleasantness, etc,
that have become attached to perceptions through experience. The second
development is a differentiation of needs and interests. This has to do with
feelings of contentment, disappointment, and all gradations in between that
are not just tied to various perceptions but that are *associated with action
as a whole.* Let us begin our discussion of the affective phenomena characteristic of this period by reviewing some classical ideas about the earliest
acquired feelings.

It is generally accepted that the structure of the affective life is a form
of rhythm. Excitation alternates with depression, joy with sadness. It is
important to realize, however, that notions such as pleasure and pain are
antithetical only from the point of view of valuation. Such oppositions have
not been shown to exist from the point of view of psychophysiologic sensibility. The difference between positively and negatively valued affects may,

21

in fact, be only a difference of degree. Let us quickly consider several aspects of this problem.

The classical physiological conception of pain denied that a special sensory modality was involved. Contrary to this, von Frey and Blix (1890–1894) believed they had found "pain points" and maintained, in contrast to Wundt, the existence of a pain sense. Golscheider observed, however, that pain points do not produce a sensation of pain if they are stimulated very lightly. This inclined people to believe that pain points might be nothing more than extremely sensitive pressure points, and since that time the problem of pain has stimulated numerous discussions. These were summarized by Piéron at the Stockholm Psychology Congress in 1951. Piéron ended his analysis by refusing to make a special sense like hearing or vision out of pain. Pain was not a sensation, said Piéron, but an affective impression linked to certain categories of excitants that acted on the other senses. This meant that affective reactions involved coordinations that brought cortical sensory mechanisms into play and again indicated that a connection between affective and cognitive functions existed.

Where *pleasure* is concerned, it is also a question of an affective impression; and, in fact, an entire hierarchy of pleasures is found. This hierarchy extends from pleasures of the simplest localized physical variety up to the most complex forms of functional pleasure connected with elaborated activities like grasping or swinging an object, etc. Functional pleasures of every sort are differentiated in concert with the differentiation of actions themselves. They play a fundamental role in the acquisition of habits in general.

Pleasantness and unpleasantness are two more feelings that are difficult to analyze. Ordinarily, psychologists refuse to identify them with mild pleasures or pains because there is evidence against doing so. Some light pain, for example, may not be unpleasant. In his analytic studies on the psychology of feelings, Wundt concluded that it was necessary to add other descriptive categories such as "exciting" and "calming" or "straining" and "relaxing" to characterize feelings. The first of these pairs was supposed to be similar to what a person feels when he perceives lively or dull colors, red being exciting, gray calming. The second corresponded to the feelings that are experienced when a person follows the beats of a metronome moving at different speeds.

Considering affectivity in general, a common fault of classical psychology has been to identify "affective states" with sensations. Just as many older theories reconstructed perceptions by combining sensations, they composed "higher feelings" by associating elementary affective states in different ways. Today, thanks in particular to the work of gestalt theorists, the difference between a sensation and a perception is recognized to be a difference in the degree of complexity only. From the moment a sensation occurs, a structure with well-defined laws of organization is found. We believe that, similar to this, a structure with laws of organization exists for the simplest affective states and that all affective phenomena occur in relation to a field. In other words, there seems to us to be an affective relativity that is isomorphic with the relativity of perceptions. Both are linked to repetition, to figure-background contrast, etc. To illustrate this, recall that one piece of cream pie may be agreeable, a second sickening, or that a dish will seem more pleasant if it is eaten following one less pleasant, etc.

While it is important to study the difference between interests and needs in order to complete this discussion, we delay doing so until we consider the following stage. Let us end our discussion of the first two stages with an examination of affectivity's role in cognitive acquisitions and the thesis of Philippe Malrieu.

In the course of the first two stages, we witness progressive differentiation of hereditary capabilities and schemes. Perceptions such as size or distance become more precise and differentiated. The first habits are constituted according to schemes of primary or secondary circular reaction. Behaviors appear that prepare the way for sensorimotor intelligence defined as the coordination of means in view of a set goal. An example of this type of intelligence would be a child seated in a cradle from whose top some dolls are suspended. By chance, the baby pulls a string which moves the top and makes the dolls dance in the air. This discovery amuses him. Henceforth, when he perceives a new object he pulls on the cord again in the hope of making it move even though the object may not be connected with the top. Such behavior indicates that the means of achieving a goal are differentiated from the goal itself and are coordinated around a definite purpose.[7]

From the affective point of view, inherited feelings and perceptual affects are involved in all these acquisitions. Should we say, then, that cognitive structures and the corresponding feelings that act as motivational elements are elaborated in parallel? Or does affectivity cause the creation of cognitive structures? This second hypothesis, opposed to our own, has been adopted by Philippe Malrieu (*Les émotions et la personnalité de l'enfant de la naissance à trois ans*). Let us examine his ideas.

Malrieu holds that the child's acquisitions during the first three years of life are due not only to maturation but also and especially to *activity oriented by affectivity*. For him, the term affectivity designates feelings in the broad sense; and its influence on cognition may be followed stage by stage.

On the reflex level, consolidating or inhibiting exercise takes place as a function of contentment or displeasure. Pleasure and pain are determinants,

---

[7]See the exposition and detailed study of this example in *Bulletin de Psychologie*, Vol. VI, No. 3.

and this "dynamogenic" (*dynamogénique*) is the same as "contentment." The primary circular reactions, according to Malrieu, are not due to "functional assimilation" as we suppose but to affective factors like impatience, enjoyment, discontentedness, etc. Further, Malrieu calls the secondary circular reactions "correlations" (*corrélations*) and explains them in a similar way. The constitution of objects begins when they are external to action proper, and the "separation" of self and objects is due to the "advent of desire." Finally, says Malrieu, perception of good forms is also of affective origin. A form is good not relative to the structure of a subject's sensory organs, but rather it appears or disappears as a function of the subject's affective state.

This theory appears to us to present two major difficulties. To begin with, it employs a conception of affectivity that is too general and nonspecific. Malrieu seems to confuse affectivity, which has to do with feelings and drives on every level, with emotions.[8] He does not distinguish between emotions and perceptual affects nor does he appreciate the progressive differentiation of feelings, which is seen throughout development and which is inadequately explained by maturation. Malrieu's theory of need is not acceptable for similar reasons. He denies that need might have an elemental character but speaks, rather, of "excitatory" experiences. How can an experience be excitatory in one case and not in another? To say that interest is a response to an excitant is to explain equivalent terms by one another!

The second problem with Malrieu's hypothesis is that it reduces everything to affectivity. In fact, Malrieu describes no structure at all. If contentment is the cause of action, what is the cause of contentment? How can one explain contentment on the reflex level without invoking structures, i.e. differentiated organs and instinctual organizations of behavior? The same applies on the level of circular reactions. Malrieu claims that a child acquires a new behavior because he finds it interesting. Does this mean that the contentment the behavior procures for the child and which makes it interesting came before the behavior, itself, and caused its acquisition? In the example of the baby who pulls the string, how would one explain the infant's enjoyment without presupposing the perception and comprehension of certain relationships and how would the "pleasure" taken in such relationships be explained? How, moreover, could the "pleasure of being the cause" be accounted for without presupposing cognitive structure in the

---

[8]See footnote 5. In this case, it is impossible to omit the reference to emotion and still retain Piaget's argument. In the deleted section on emotion Piaget classified emotions as instinctual. They were, therefore, limited to Stage I. From that point of view, to confuse feelings and emotivity (emotional expression), as Piaget holds Malrieu does, is to confuse the affective manifestations of several levels with those found on a single level.—Translators

form of some scheme of "causality?" Malrieu does not furnish satisfactory responses to these questions.

In our view, it is dangerous to start off by dissociating behavior into two aspects, affective and cognitive, and then to make one the cause of the other. Understanding is no more the cause of affectivity than affectivity is the cause of understanding. Energetics cannot generate structures nor structures create energy. Failure to understand the concomitant indissociability and fundamental heterogeneity of cognition and affectivity leads to paradoxical explanations. A case in point would be Malrieu's explanation of how self and objects become separated by "the advent of desire." This implies that awareness of the separation is due to desire whereas, to our way of thinking, there is desire only because there is perception of the separation. This does not mean, however, that the distance perceived is the cause of the desire felt. It means, rather, that obstacles to the satisfaction of needs *simultaneously* lead to intellectual differentiation, in this case perception of distance, and to affective differentiation, in this case unsatisfied desire.

For his part, Malrieu reproaches us for explaining everything by intelligence. Let us respond only that this reproach would be perfectly sound if we had begun by making two distinct factors of cognition and affectivity and then had made the first determine the second. It would have meaning only if a preexisting dualism of this sort had been posited. The psychology of intelligence does not presuppose a dualism of any kind, however. By definition, cognitive psychology studies intellectual structures; it in no way claims to account for every aspect of behavior. It is Malrieu, in fact, who falls into the dualistic error and who reverts to what almost amounts to "facultative psychology" by making affectivity the *cause* of behavior.

In conclusion, we again stress our belief that there is a constant and dialectic interaction between affectivity and intelligence. Both are developed and transformed in interconnected ways as a function of the progressive organization of behavior, but one is not caused by the other. The psychologist artificially separates them for convenience of exposition. He must demonstrate that they are different in nature without, for all that, dichotomizing behavior and refusing to recognize its concrete unity. Moreover, he must avoid making a *deus ex machina* of maturation by invoking its action without sufficient physiological facts. When maturation is made a "cause," the problem is often only displaced. Maturation is not, by itself, the cause of anything. It is limited to specifying the field of possibilities belonging to a given level.

THIRD STAGE: AFFECTS REGULATING INTENTIONAL BEHAVIOR

The third stage includes substages IV–VI of the sensorimotor intelligence. It is marked by the appearance of intelligent acts, properly so-called, and involves complex affective as well as cognitive coordinations and regulations. We shall study the principal features of both.

From the cognitive perspective, the characteristics of this stage include the differentiation of means from goals and, correlative to this, the flexible coordination of means in order to achieve a goal that has been previously determined. Let us take the example of a child struggling to obtain a distant object sitting on his blanket. Not succeeding directly, he pulls on the blanket in order to bring the object closer. This indicates that during the third stage the means, or, in this case, the blanket, can be distinguished from the goal or object that the child desires. It also indicates that the child has the ability to combine behaviors he has previously acquired in different ways in order to achieve a desired goal. It is this second characteristic that, in our opinion, defines the beginning of intelligent acts.

From the affective point of view, the characteristics of the third stage also include differentiations and the beginning of decentration. The first of these is limited to the intra-individual plane and is evident in the way a child begins to coordinate his interests. In the context of intentional action, certain objects, without interest in themselves, take on interest in relation to other objects which are valued. In other words, the value of the means is determined in relation to the value of a particular goal, and labile hierarchies of values arise from activity of this sort. With the beginning of affective decentration, feelings begin to be directed toward other people in so far as the baby becomes capable of distinguishing them from himself.

Janet's Theory

Let us begin our discussion by studying Pierre Janet's theory of behavioral regulations. This was discussed briefly earlier in the course, but now it takes on special importance because it introduces us to the study of interests and values. This study leads us to the theories of Claparède and to Kurt Lewin's gestaltist notion of the affective field. Finally, we examine the theories of Freud on unconscious affective regulations and object choice as they relate to the origin of interpersonal feelings.

In the second volume of *De l'angoisse à l'extase*, Janet described a hierarchy of increasingly complex behaviors that corresponded to successive developmental stages. These included reflexes, first habits, the beginning of language, practical intelligence, etc. Janet called these behaviors "primary actions" and characterized them from the cognitive point of view. Each of them, he said, goes through four successive phases, i.e. latency, triggering, activation, and termination. The last of these constituted a consummation phase which led to a new latency phase. Janet also remarked that certain circumstances such as simplicity, familiarity of the situation, existence of internal capabilities, or external assistance could facilitate primary actions and that other circumstances such as the complexity of the task, novelty of the problem, demand for speed, absence of aids, or presence of obstacles could make them more difficult. Finally, he said, there were circumstances such as desire or ardor that could reinforce the primary action.

What was important from the affective point of view, according to Janet, were the subject's reactions to his primary actions. These "secondary actions" were, Janet argued, regulators of the primary actions. Their role was to increase or decrease the force of behavior and finally to terminate it. Janet carefully demonstrated that a behavior was not sufficient in itself but required either positive or negative regulations in the activation and termination phases. He believed four regulations of this sort could be distinguished.

The first two of Janet's secondary actions were the positive and negative *activation regulations*. The positive variety consisted of "feeling pressured"[9] and the negative variety of "feeling unpressured." The prototype

[9]The cognates of Janet's terms, *pression* and *dépression*, create confusion. In English, people speak of feeling "pressured" to do something, but they do not speak of feeling "unpressured" as being "depressed." The words, pressured and unpressured, which are used here do not avoid other ambiguities, however. For example, Janet uses the feeling of effort to illustrate the positive activation regulations while most psychologists distinguish feeling pressured from the feeling of effort. The first corresponds to the feeling that a thing has to be done immediately, the second to the difficulty felt while doing it. It is also difficult to see opposition between effort and fatigue or effort and disinterest as Janet's terms suggest one should. A person can feel fatigued, pressured to accomplish something, and experience the effort that an action takes all at once. The oppositions that suggest themselves in English would be "pressured" vs "unpressured;" "effort" vs "ease;" "interest" vs "disinterest;" "energy" vs "fatigue." Seeing no generic term for pressured, effort, interest, and energy, nor any for unpressured, ease, disinterest, and fatigue, we have translated *sentiments de pression* as "feeling pressured" and *sentiments de dépression* as "feeling unpressured," while acknowledging that this solution does not resolve every difficulty.—Translators

of the positive activation regulations was, for Janet, the feeling of *effort*. This accelerated or reinforced the primary action. Negative activation regulations braked primary action. As examples of such feelings, Janet mentioned fatigue and disinterest. The third and fourth varieties of Janet's secondary actions were the positive and negative *termination regulations*. The first of these, called by Janet "feelings of elation," terminated action by consuming forces that remained unused after success had been achieved. Examples were joy, the feeling of triumph, etc. Feelings corresponding to the negative termination regulations were sadness, anguish, anxiety, etc. It should be noted in passing that although Janet's termination regulations are observed in the secondary circular reactions of the second developmental stage and play an important role in the infant's initial acquisition of habits (Law of Effect), we study them in the third stage because they are fully developed only during that stage.

Let us focus first on Janet's proposition that the model for positive activation regulations is the feeling of effort. It is well known that Maine de Biran, writing as much from a philosophical point of view as from a psychological one, ascribed primary importance to this feeling. He saw in effort the primitive fact of inner sensibility. He believed it simultaneously and immediately gave consciousness of the self (motor term) and of the non-self (resistant term). De Biran's ingenious theory runs into two essential difficulties, however.

Consciousness of the self is not, from the genetic point of view, contemporaneous with motor action on objects. The newborn has no consciousness of himself. A two month old baby whose hand is shaken by another person looks at it with interest only if it enters his visual field by chance. Facts of this sort indicate quite clearly that the infant does not have immediate consciousness of his body as such. There is, then, all the more reason to believe that he cannot discern what belongs to him and what belongs to the external world in a "state of consciousness." Related to this is Baldwin's demonstration that consciousness of the self makes a quite tardy appearance and is constructed correlatively, not with consciousness of objects, but with consciousness of other people which comes later. All of this leads one to believe that there is no differentiation of the self and the non-self at the beginning. The primitive fact of inner sensibility cannot, therefore, be immediate consciousness of a duality.

The second difficulty facing Maine de Biran's notion of effort stems from his contention that the feeling of effort follows a centrifugal course. This point has never been proved. William James even held the opposite, i.e. that the feeling of effort arose from taking consciousness of peripheral tension and that, consequently, it followed a centripetal course.

Janet did not take a stand on these problems. The particular mechanism of effort was not important to him. For him, the essential thing was not to study emotion as a form of consciousness but to study it as a form of behavior. As we have said, Janet envisioned emotion as an energetic regulation reinforcing or accelerating primary action. The child who unsuccessfully tries to reach a distant object with a stick will stretch his arm further. The feeling of effort provides supplemental energy which increases the intensity and amplitude of the primary action. Other secondary actions such as attention and, more generally, all activities that are centered on a particularly interesting object can be found.

A final observation on Janet's notion of positive activation regulations is that they are susceptible to derangement. They may extend past useful functioning and become excessive. Recall in this connection the celebrated analyses that Janet made of worry or boredom. These, he said, were not feelings stemming from exhaustion but were, instead, precautionary behaviors which acted against excessive positive activation. Boredom was not a behavior found in worn-out subjects. It was behavior that allowed mental "tonus" to be conserved.

In general, Janet's negative activation regulations corresponded to feeling unpressured. These were secondary actions whose effect was to slow down the action undertaken. They were manifested as decreases in intensity or speed, as restrictions of the field of action, or as what Janet called "devaluations." By this latter term, he meant diminution of the pleasure taken in an action. Janet said that feeling unpressured was manifested on the sensorimotor level by the child's gravity (*le sérieux de l'enfant*). The prototype of this was, for Janet, the feeling of fatigue. If physiological fatigue was the consequence of muscular effort, the feeling of fatigue, he said, was a behavior that stopped action before the subject ran out of strength. It was an anticipatory regulation permitting energy to be saved. Thanks to fatigue, action would be able to continue at a later time. If fatigue had not set in at the appropriate moment, the subject, instead of stopping, would have expended his remaining strength and become exhausted.

Now let us consider Janet's termination regulations. Action, Janet noted, did not stop all by itself. Special behavior, positive or negative, was required to terminate it. In case of failure, action was terminated by a feeling of sadness which was, for Janet, very different from the feeling of fatigue. Sadness was a differentiated behavior that occurred after an action was completed. Whereas fatigue acted to save energy, as we saw earlier, the function of sadness was to consume the residue of unused forces. Consummation behaviors were also found when an act turned out well. These, too, expended what was left of the forces mobilized for action. The affective aspect of these behaviors was the feeling of triumph, etc.

In certain cases, Janet believed negative termination regulations could be excessive and bring about a retreat from previously attained levels of functioning. Sadness, for example, could be prolonged into anxiety and result in withdrawal from activity since the subject no longer dared to start again. Janet's and Freud's theories might even by reconciled on this point. Janet's sadness would terminate Freud's parapraxes (*actes manqués*); and the same could be said for anxiety, which Freud explained by a repression of the libido and which Janet extended as a secondary regulation to all of conduct.

In summary, Janet's central idea was that of a "psychological force" the nature of which was poorly understood. From the physiological point of view, this force supposedly depended on vegetative functioning, on the endocrine system, etc. What the psychologist observed, according to Janet, was that psychological force was distributed differently in different individuals and even within the same individual from one moment to another. Everyone, he remarked, experienced alternations of strength and weakness, of euphoria and depression, and these might even go as far as cyclothymia in certain individuals. In every behavior, reserve force had to be used and the energy expended had to be recovered. One way the latter could be accomplished was to produce a lowering of psychological tension. All of this, in Janet's view, indicated the essential role that *regulations* played in the general economics of behavior. Behavior always tended towards an equilibrium of one kind or another, and it always involved four conditions:

1. The regulations enumerated above,
2. Forces in reserve,
3. A proportionality between available forces and psychological tension which determined the level of activity,
4. A relationship between previous actions and new ones which involved adaptation and effort.

Variable according to the individual, affective equilibrium was also variable with respect to age. It was precarious in the child whose feelings were very strong but whose behavior alternated constantly. In older people, behavior was more stable but feelings lost their vivacity. In Janet's theory, the intensity of feelings was, therefore, a function of disequilibrium.

Critique of Janet's Theory

The first point to be made in critically evaluating Janet's theory is that although all of Janet's analyses are acceptable from our point of view, we question whether all affective phenomena can be reduced to the energetic regulations he describes. There is no doubt about the regulatory role of feelings. It seems, however, that a second regulatory system must be added to Janet's system of secondary actions. This second system would have to do with interest and the evaluation of action. Why this is necessary is best seen by examining Janet's remarks regarding the third condition of equilibrium listed above. According to Janet, the proportionality between available forces and psychological tension or, in other words, the balancing of the cost of the means needed to achieve some goal with the value of the goal itself was ruled by a principle of subsequent savings. There were actions that are costly to carry out, said Janet, but whose effects would permit psychological force or energy to be saved later. We would say, instead, that it is necessary to distinguish between the value of an action and its cost. A costly action may be preferred to one that costs less but that the subject also values less. Valuation is not the simple consequence of the economics of behavior.

In order to illustrate this point, let us take the example of a child of thirteen months who tries in vain to bring a long slender toy into his playpen by pulling it through the bars in a horizontal position. This is a classic instance of a problem of practical intelligence that is solved by groping. By chance, the child succeeds in turning the toy into the vertical position and in pulling it through the bars. Instead of being content with this success, however, he again puts the toy outside the playpen and recommences his gropings until he has understood the technique. This searching on the baby's part seems to run counter to the principle of economy of action.

Janet does not overlook the fact that such behaviors exist; but, as indicated above, he attempts to reduce them to his energetic system by saying that this costly choice of actions will represent a subsequent saving of energy. This would obviously not be so in the example just cited. The value that the baby places on bringing the object through the bars of his playpen has nothing to do with saving energy. If it did, he would not repeat the same action over and over but would be content once the object was through the bars. For this reason, it is necessary to suppose that something other than an internal regulation of forces is involved. The notion of value must be brought into play. What is important to the baby and the reason that he starts all over is that he is interested in expanding his activity and his sense of self through his conquest of the universe. This expansion involves assimilation, understanding, etc. From this point of view, value is an affective exchange with the exterior, i.e. with objects or people. It comes into play even in primary actions, and the system of values goes beyond the simply energetic regulatory system of secondary actions described by Janet. In order to understand this, the notions of value and interest are studied next.

The Notions of Value and Interest

To start with, we define value as a general dimension of affectivity and not as a particular and privileged feeling. The problem is to know when valuation is involved and why. We have said that valuation cannot be explained as a simple "economy for what follows" and that the system of values goes beyond Janet's system of affective regulations. At the stage under consideration, however, the distinction between values and energetic regulations is only beginning to appear. Despite this apparent initial fusion, we have argued that values play a distinct role in primary actions and are evident from the moment the subject begins to relate to the external world. In learning to walk, for example, previous success or failure can be seen to influence the child's interest and endeavor. This clearly indicates that some sort of self-estimation is taking place. As early as the sensorimotor level, then, the child draws not only practical knowledge but also confidence in or doubt about himself from previous experience. These feelings are, in a way, analogous to feelings of superiority or inferiority (but with the careful qualification that the self is not yet constituted in the early sensorimotor substages). They will play a large part in determining the finality of action proper and soon will be extended to all of the interpersonal relationships that appear with imitatory behaviors. As values attributed to people, the elementary forms of which are liking (*sympathie*) and disliking (*antipathie*), these feelings become the starting point for moral feelings. One sees, therefore, that values, although difficult to discern at first, are organized bit by bit into a system that is broader, more stable, and distinct from the system of energetic regulations.

The two systems of which we speak, i.e. valuation and internal regulation, find their juncture in the mechanism of interest. Our first approach to this idea is to study the work of Claparède (cf *Psychologie de l'enfant et pédagogie expérimentale,* 2nd ed., 1909, revised and developed in various later works). Claparède defined *interest* as a regulation of energies in a sense very akin to that of Janet. It was, he said, the relation between a need and an object capable of satisfying that need. For Claparède, neither the object nor the need sufficed to determine what behavior a person would undertake. It was necessary to insert a third term, which was the relationship between these two.

Need can be studied from the physiological point of view. Certain writers attribute a peripheral origin to it, others a central origin. Claparède, like Janet, did not think that that was the most important aspect of the problem, however. He stressed its functional significance. Need manifested disequilibrium, and the satisfaction of a need signified re-equilibration.

In order to clarify the notion of *equilibrium*, let us recall that three types may be distinguished. First of all, there is mechanical equilibrium which has to do with systems where potential modifications compensate one another under stable and permanent conditions. The second sort of equilibrium is physicochemical in nature and occurs under nonpermanent conditions that may lead to displacements of the equilibrium. It involves compensation in the sense that real rather than potential modifications of the system are balanced. This form of equilibrium obeys Le Châtelier's Law, a principle that often has been revived by biologists and psychologists. Finally, there is organic equilibrium which is comparable to Cannon's homeostasis and which involves compensations before the fact or anticipatory regulations.

Many needs appear in advance of actual physiological disequilibrium. Claparède demonstrated this with regard to sleep, a subject strongly debated in his time. Most authors then writing explained sleep as an effect of metabolic intoxication. Claparède raised three objections to this idea. First, he said, people slept before they were physiologically intoxicated, and in any case, intoxication induced insomnia not sleep. Second, Claparède objected, there existed an instinctive sleep such as one saw in dormice and woodchucks. Third, he pointed out that there was a kind of sleep that resulted from disinterest and not from physiological intoxication. All these arguments led him to see the need to sleep as an anticipatory regulation and not the result of physiological disequilibrium.

Claparède also held that organic needs, properly speaking, e.g. hunger and thirst, could be distinguished from derived needs, the latter being more or less complex mixtures of organic needs. For our purposes, it will be sufficient to indicate only that, for Claparède, every need was linked to an organic structure whose functioning created new structures in response to certain disequilibria. There was, therefore, a constant dialectical exchange between needs and functions.

This preliminary analysis of need was used by Claparède to justify two *laws of interest.* The first of these stated that all behavior was dictated by interest. The second posited that there could be several interests in play at the same instant. According to Claparède's theory, the organism acted in accordance with its greatest interest. He also pointed out that the same object could be used differently according to the interest of the moment. The bottle had interest for the baby to the extent that he was hungry. In cases such as this, rhythms of interest could be distinguished.

Finally, Claparède distinguished two meanings of interest. On the one hand, interest was the "dynamogenerator" (*dynamogénisateur*) of action. Objects of interest liberated energy whereas those of no interest inhibited the expenditure of energy. This was the regulatory aspect of interest. On the other hand, Claparède held that interest was related to the *finality of action* because the choice of objects corresponded to the satisfaction desired. This distinction is important because these two meanings correspond to the two systems we are trying to distinguish.[10] The first has to do with the *intensity*

[10]A line is missing from the French original. The words "these two meanings correspond to" have been added.—Translators

of interest, i.e. its quantitative aspect, and involves the regulation of energy or force. The second has to do with the *content of interest*, i.e. its qualitative aspect. This has to do with the values relative to which means and ends will be distributed.

The elementary interests found in children are linked to fundamental organic needs. They are progressively interwoven into complex systems as the child grows up. Much later they will be intellectualized and become scales of values. We shall have occasion in what follows to study the intellectualization and stabilization of such systems. For the moment, let us limit ourselves to recognizing that interest represents the point of juncture between two distinct systems. It is where the system of valuation and the system of energetic regulation come together.

Now let us turn to an analysis quite different from Claparède's but one in which we again find a distinction between two systems. Kurt Lewin began with gestalt theory, which had stressed the importance of equilibrium and disequilibrium in perceptual structures. Lewin applied these concepts to the problems of affective psychology. In doing so, he extended the notion of *field* from the poorly structured perceptual field . . . and finally the self itself.[11] Let us examine his ideas briefly.

In Lewin's theory there was no discontinuity between perceptual and motor structures. Motor activity could restore equilibrium in a poorly structured perceptual field. If, for example, a single object appeared in the middle of an empty perceptual field, there was equilibrium, stability, and immobility. If, on the other hand, the object appeared at the periphery of the perceptual field, the field's structure became asymmetrical and equilibrium would be re-established by displacement of the eyes and head. From the structural or cognitive viewpoint, therefore, the field included both perceptual structure, properly so-called, and motor structures. Lewin believed that it was necessary to add a dynamic aspect to this structural aspect, however. He did this by postulating that the self made up part of the *total field* and that because of this the analysis of behavior brought up structural and dynamic problems simultaneously. As an example of the dynamic aspect, Lewin cited the motives that instigate the subject's action. The notion of *need* corresponded to the gestalt concept of the "character of solicitation." It was understood, however, that need or solicitation depended neither on the object's structure (*praegnanz*) alone nor on the subject's inclinations only. It depended on the configuration of the total field.

[11]A second line is missing from the French original. Apparently this detailed the constitutents of Lewin's extended field which lay between "the poorly structured perceptual field" and "the self." In this case, nothing has been added. The components of Lewin's total field are listed subsequently in the text.—Translators

It remains to be determined whether these ideas agree with the distinction we have made between the valuation system and the system of energetic regulation. In this regard, let us recall two of Lewin's experiments. The first of these concerned the influence of affective reactions on the way children solve problems of practical intelligence. A child was placed in a circle drawn on the floor with chalk and was forbidden to cross it. At the same time, he was instructed to obtain an object placed outside the circle beyond his reach. He had different sorts of intermediaries such as sticks, strings, etc, at his disposal. Lewin interpreted the situation dynamically. Because of its desirability, the object to be obtained constituted an attractive force. The circle of chalk and the instruction not to cross it constituted a "psychic barrier" or negative force. The disequilibrium between these two forces caused tension which the child tried to resolve through different behaviors. Either he would cross the circle and appropriate the object, thereby achieving only partial satisfaction since he had not followed directions; or he would respect the instructions without obtaining the object; or he would remain immobile and would no longer seek a solution; or he would reject the problem and would play with an object in the circle of chalk, etc. In short, besides successful solutions, a whole series of behaviors and corresponding feelings was observed. The feelings were determined by the variable equilibrium of the forces opposing one another in the total field. In addition, Lewin demonstrated how previous successes and failures modified the value the child placed on the task by increasing or decreasing his *level of aspiration* (*Anspruchs*-level). Presentation of analogous or novel tasks demonstrated that the subject engaged himself in different degrees according to the success or failure of previous attempts.

The second of Lewin's experiments had to do with interrupted tasks (Zeigarnik and Lewin). Subjects were presented with various problems of practical intelligence. Some were allowed to complete their task while others were interrupted under a plausible pretext. At the end of twenty-four hours, an analysis was made to determine what remained in the subject's mind relative to the finished and unfinished actions. It was found that interrupted actions left a *quasi-need*, i.e. a tendency to complete the task. What Janet would call a termination regulation was lacking.

We retain the following from Kurt Lewin's psychology:

1. The importance accorded the *structure of the total field* with interdependence between the subject and the objective configuration of the field,
2. The *dynamic polarization of the field* whose structure is expressed in vector terminology and gives place to a sort of subjective geometry or "hodological topology,"
3. The importance accorded the *subject's previous activity*.

The last of these is important because, in general, classical gestaltists underestimated the subject's activity and neglected the influence of previous experience. This third element of Lewin's theory fills in this lacuna and brings out the historical character of behavior. No longer is the field defined only in terms of its spatial configuration. *Its structure is spatiotemporal.* When successive trials are observed, the magnitude of a psychic barrier varies. It is from this spatiotemporal point of view that we again discover the system of regulations and the system of valuation. To the *spatial,* i.e. simultaneous, current, and synchronic, *aspect* correspond behaviors that arise directly from the *system of regulations.* To the *temporal aspect* corresponds the *system of values* dependent on the subject's history. We conclude this part of our discussion, then, by clearly stating the proposed distinction in terms of fields. The value system is essentially *diachronic* in contrast to the *synchronic* system regulating forces.

Affective Decentration and the Problem of "Object Choice"

The characteristics of the third stage that have been considered so far have been the differentiation of means from goals, the energetic regulations of intentional sensorimotor behaviors, and the beginning hierarchization of values. There is another important development in this period, however. Specifically, it is during this stage that other people begin to be appreciated as such and, consequently, that the first forms of interpersonal feelings begin. Affectivity, which up until this time had been centered on a self undifferentiated from external objects or other people, will begin to be decentered. We must try to understand how the child makes the transition from intra-individual affectivity of the sort seen in the previous stages to interpersonal affectivity bearing on distinct external objects and a clearly defined self. We must also attempt to understand the connection that exists between sensorimotor intelligence and this differentiated affectivity. This is the problem Freud called "object choice." Our discussion of this topic again illustrates the parallelism between affective and intellectual development.

Freud introduced several fertile concepts into affective psychology which have become firmly established by the success of psychoanalysis. Let us begin by reviewing Freud's schema, the simplicity and coherence of which are particularly noteworthy. At the same time, let us try to understand the inadequacies of Freud's hypothesis that make it unable to account for certain aspects of affective evolution.

We begin by questioning how feelings develop during exchanges such as smiling at or playing with other people. Are the feelings involved in some way "innate" and is affective development only a matter of transferring these inborn feelings from one object to another? Or do new feelings which were not present at birth arise as products of genuine construction? Let us take the case of attachment to the mother. It can easily be imagined that such feelings correspond to instinctual drives. The behaviors by which they are expressed are, however, very different in children of three weeks, two months, or two years. How can these transformations be explained? Two antithetical solutions are possible. On the one hand, one can propose an instinct that remains identical to itself (libido) and that is transformed by successive changes in the object to which it is attached (transference). On the other hand, one can propose a series of constructions properly so-called.

The first solution is the Freudian one. Alongside the "self-drives" (*Ichtriebe*), which are preservation instincts having to do with the subject himself, exist the "sexual drives" (*Sexualtriebe*). The *sexual drives* are present from the start, are permanent, and are conserved from stage to stage. Their objective changes in the course of development, however, and these *transferences* constitute the criterion that distinguishes the different stages of affective life. During the child's first years, one can distinguish three phases of this sort. The first phase is that in which the libido is focused only on the subject's body. This is called the digestive stage. Quite soon peripheral differentiations appear giving rise to oral and anal stages. In the second phase, the libido bears on the subject's *activity* in general. This is the stage of primary narcissism. Finally, the third phase is characterized by the transference of affectivity onto external objects such as other people and especially the mother. This transference of affectivity onto objects gives rise to interpersonal feelings, complexes, etc.

According to Freudian theory, memories of previous stages are *repressed* when libidinal displacements cause entry into a new stage. Such memories, only being repressed, do not disappear and may resurface if regression takes place. Displacement and correlative repression constitute, therefore, the mechanism of the successive affective transformations.

Seductive as this explanation is, it does not account for all the facts or for every aspect of affective development. Freud was particularly preoccupied with explaining adult affectivity and regression to infantile stages. One result of this is that his work is not developmental enough. He imagines that the child has mental functions before the appearance of language that, in fact, only develop afterward. More generally, he neglects considering affective and intellectual development in parallel even though it is particularly important to do so.

Let us begin by critically examining his concept of repression. Today this concept is universally accepted. Freud first described it as a mechanism that submerges affects and drives in the unconscious where they continue to "live" and be transformed. The original conception of repression was, however, rapidly broadened by Freud and his disciples. Pfister compared repression to the inhibition of drives which can be experimentally demonstrated in animals. An example would be Möbius' pike. Möbius demonstrated that if a pike was put into an aquarium with a carp but was separated from it by a plate of glass, the pike would give up attacking the carp after several collisions with the glass. If the glass was then removed, the pike still did not attack the carp even though it was no longer separated from it. From data of this sort, Pfister reasoned that the notion of repression might be broadened to include reflexive inhibition. In our opinion, Freud made too liberal use of this interesting idea, and his theory is not equal to the established facts. As mentioned above, Freud used repression to explain the fact that there are no memories of the first year of life. It seems more likely, however, that this lack of memories reflects the simple fact that the young infant does not have evocative memory, which presupposes representation and the symbolic function, rather than that he has such memories but represses them.

An analogous criticism can be made with respect to *narcissism*. Narcissism cannot be conceived as a focusing of affectivity on the subject's own activity or as self-contemplation precisely at a time when the self is not yet formed. Narcissism is affectivity corresponding to the lack of differentiation of the self from the non-self (Baldwin's "adualistic state" or Wallon's "affective symbiosis"). The infant's primary narcissism is a narcissism without a Narcissus. It is correlative to a non-spatialized causality without contact with the physical world. It is the affective analogue of behavior of the sort where a child who is shown how a light switch works subsequently opens and closes his eyes in front of the switch. Such behavior indicates that the child in no way differentiates between the light-to-dark transition that results from an external modification (light switch) and that which results from opening and closing his eyes. We contend that the symmetry that is evident between affective narcissism and intellectual egocentrism is another instance of the general *symmetry* between affectivity and intelligence.

The most important problem, however, is the transition from primary narcissism to *object choice.* [12] Two interpretations are possible. On the one hand, we might imagine that the child perceives objects as we perceive them. In that case, the child's perceptual pictures, like an adult's, would be filled with solid and permanent objects. People would only be special objects because they are the source of more numerous satisfactions or threats. The

[12]*Object choice* is a psychoanalytic term and is intended here in its technical psychoanalytic meaning. Although Freud was later to deny the existence of primary narcissism, in the conception of object choice to which Piaget refers object choice involves the conversion of narcissistic libido stored in the ego into object libido centered on another person. It should be noted that the word object refers to a person in psychoanalytic contexts of this sort whereas for Piaget it refers to all physical objects including other people as well as one's own body.
—Translators

transition from primary narcissism to object choice would be accomplished by transferring libido from the subject's body onto others (displacement). The second possibility would be to suppose that the child initially inhabits a universe without objects. Object choice would then imply construction of the object.

The first of these interpretations is the Freudian one. The second is the interpretation we shall make. What, in effect, is an object? It is a poly-sensorial complex which continues to exist apart from all perceptual contact. We recognize schemes of objects in an infant's sensorimotor reactions through the characteristics of *solidity* (the object lasts longer than the corresponding perception) and *localization* (the object exists in space apart from the perceptual field). These characteristics represent two complementary aspects of the same behavioral system. Nothing in the baby's initial actions justifies belief in the presence of constituted objects. While it is true that the child has recognitive memory much before it has evocative memory, the fact that a baby recognizes things does not prove the existence of objects as defined above. Nor does the fact that the gaze follows a displaced object imply solidity; it is only a continuation of the action in progress.

Experiments support these interpretations. From four and one half months onward the baby can coordinate his prehensile movements with his perceptions. He tries to grasp what he sees, hears, or feels. If he is shown an interesting object, he stretches out his arm to grab it. If at that moment the object is covered by a screen, the baby withdraws his hand. Around six months, there is evidence of progress, but the object is still not definitively constituted. To demonstrate this, two screens, A and B, are used. The object is hidden behind A in a conspicuous way. The infant removes A and finds it. The object is next hidden behind B. The infant, however, picks up A again and not finding the object stops what he is doing. This experiment indicates that there is a beginning of object solidification since the baby attempts to find the displaced object, but it also demonstrates that objects are not yet localized since they are not sought as a function of their displacements. If localization is made the criterion for the presence of objects, objects cannot exist before space is structured in such a way that combinations of movements, reverse movements, and detours lead back to the starting point. In other words, localization requires space to be organized into a "group of displacements."

If there are no objects in the beginning but only moving perceptual pictures and if an object's existence requires that it be constructed in concert with the structuration of space, then affective object choice is no longer simply a choice among already structured objects brought about simply by transferring libido. Object choice becomes one aspect of the baby's elaboration of the universe. It involves both *cognitive decentration* with elaboration of external space and *affective decentration* manifested as interest in sources of pleasure henceforth conceived to be distinct from the subject's own actions. From the moment that such decentrations become possible, exchange relationships between the subject and the external world will replace symbiotic relationships; and those exchanges will have affective as well as cognitive aspects. Critical evaluation of the Freudian explanation leads us to speak, therefore, not of an "affective object choice" but of both affective and cognitive elaborations of the object.

Let us now outline the principle aspects of these elaborations. From the cognitive point of view, five correlative and contemporaneous transformations are observed in the elaboration of the object. The first of these has to do with the construction of objects properly so-called. This occurs in connection with the structuration of space and involves localization and coordination of successive displacements into a group.[13] The object is constituted as a permanent element independent of the perceptual experience by which it is discovered.

The second transformation is the objectification and spatialization of causality. Up to this time, causality had remained linked to action with no differentiation between what resulted from action and what resulted from things. In this regard, recall the example cited previously of the infant who pulled a string fastened to the top of his crib in order to make things move, even those not connected with his crib. In that example, the cause was the subject's action and the effects were the object's movements. By contrast, during the period we are presently considering, the baby's actions and reactions indicate that he knows an object can be the cause of another object's displacements without his own action being involved at all. He also understands, in terms of sensorimotor schemes, that all causation requires spatial contact.

The third transformation is one in which people acquire the same characteristics objects have. In other words, people also become objectified and spatialized. Prior to this people had been only momentary perceptual entities which were not localized in space after they disappeared. They now become permanent objects which are localizable even when they escape perception. At the same time, they become autonomous sources of causality.

The fourth transformation with which we are concerned has to do with changes seen in the baby's imitation of others. Imitation is meant in the strict sense of the term, i.e. in the sense of a systematic effort to copy new

[13]Piaget is referring to his theory of how space is constructed. The term group is intended in its logical or mathematical sense and refers to Poincaré's "practical group of spatial displacements." See Jean Piaget and Barbel Inhelder, *The Psychology of the Child* (New York: Basic Books, 1969).—Translators

gestures from a model. Imitative behaviors appear quite early but are only progressively elaborated. Three stages can be distinguished: sporadic imitation in the form of contagion, imitation of familiar models in opposition to new models, and systematic imitation of new models with unfamiliar features. The last of these, among other things, allows the baby to establish correspondences between visible parts of another person's body, particularly the face, and the parts of his own body which he knows tactilely but not visually. Through this type of imitation the baby gains deeper knowledge of his body.

The fifth and last transformation occurs in the subject's taking consciousness of himself and his own activity. As Baldwin has clearly shown, this can be done only correlatively to taking consciousness of others. It is only when the external world is structured that consciousness of the self, consciousness of others, and consciousness of analogies between the self and others simultaneously appear.

From the affective point of view, these findings suggest that the displacement of activity and affectivity onto others, a displacement that frees the child from his narcissism, is much more than a transference, pure and simple. It is a restructuration of the entire affective and cognitive universe. When another person becomes an independent, permanent, and autonomous object, self-other relationships are no longer simple relationships between the subject's activity and an external object. These relationships start to become true exchange relationships between the self and the other person (alter ego). These exchanges make more important, more structured, and more stable valuations possible. Such valuations indicate the beginning of interpersonal "moral feelings." We study them in more detail in the following stages.

Finally, the fact that these two constructions, affective and cognitive, are simultaneous must be stressed again. There is no reason to separate intelligence from affectivity, nor is it necessary to ask which of the two precedes and conditions the other. It is a matter of two inseparable aspects of mental development. Nevertheless, many Freudians contend that affective evolution is primordial and orients intellectual evolution while others maintain that behaviors such as those seen in the third stage indicate that cognitive mechanisms like perception and structuration determine affectivity. In our view, however, both of these alternatives distort the problem. This is because there are not two developments, one cognitive and the other affective, nor are there two separate psychological functions or two sorts of objects. All objects are simultaneously cognitive and affective. Other people are simultaneously objects of knowledge and objects of affection just as, in the experiment described above, the object hidden behind a screen is both an object of knowledge, since it appears in and then disappears from the perceptual field, and a source of interest, amusement, satisfaction, or disappointment depending on whether or not the baby finds it. The two aspects are constantly complementary.

We believe that so far we have demonstrated in a satisfactory way just how artificial and untrue any explanation of cognitive development by affectivity would be or vice versa. Let us return to this question one more time, however, in order to do justice to a last possible objection. Specifically, we refer to the question of whether or not the recent works on hospitalism justify the psychoanalytic theses. Some people claim that these studies demonstrate that the affective frustrations of babies who are separated from their mothers cause retardations or disturbances in intellectual development. We disagree with this for the following reasons. On the one hand, Spitz and his collaborators have clearly demonstrated the existence of individual reactions which vary from one baby to another depending on the child's hereditary constitution and, even more importantly, on whether it was reared in a normal family, prison nursery, or foundling home, etc. This aspect of the problem arises from differential psychology, however, and not from general psychology with which we are exclusively concerned. On the other hand, Spitz has established developmental retardation in cases of "hospitalism." The fact that there are disturbances in cognitive structures that correspond to disturbances in the energetic or affective side of behavior does not insure that the latter has caused the former, however. Lacking necessary environmental stimulation, there is general developmental retardation. Unfavorable conditions impede functioning and lead to functional regressions, both cognitive and affective, but neither type of regression causes the other.

Conclusion

We end our study of the third stage at this point. This stage sees the flowering of sensorimotor intelligence characterized by the subordination of means to the goal pursued. Complex behaviors appear on the cognitive plane; new forms of feeling show up on the affective. Feelings linked to the regulation and coordination of action are characteristic of this stage. These we described along the lines of Janet, Claparède, and Lewin. Even more characteristic of this stage, however, is the appearance of a value system which is not just a matter of the economy of action but which has to do with its finality. This value system determines the energies employed in action. It was extracted not just from current behavior but also from behaviors that have come before. As values are accorded to actions and to other people, they come to play a considerable role in the subsequent development of feelings.

Value, we said, is difficult to define at the stage considered here. An object or person has value vis-à-vis the subject's action. In a sense then, values *enrich* action. This may be in terms of force; but more than anything else, it is a functional enrichment in that valued objects or people provide the subject with new goals. In what follows, we see the value system become more specific and more stable. It begins to last beyond behaviors of immediate interest to the subject and eventually defines the norms of action.

There is an apparent contradiction that arises from this developmental hypothesis, however. It stems from the implication that the values discussed in the present stage will eventually be transformed into "disinterested values" which do not appear to enrich the subject but, on the contrary, to require sacrifice. In other words, how can the intra-individual values involved in action give rise to reciprocal interpersonal exchanges, which are not a simple gift-for-gift affair? This is parallel to the situation in the cognitive domain where practical intelligence oriented towards the realization of goals is succeeded by a disinterested intelligence, representative and gnostic, presupposing decentration and aimed at understanding. In what follows, we argue that, far from contradicting our definition, reciprocal value exchanges lead to a mutual enrichment of partners through an exchange of attitudes. Affective decentration is effected through this reciprocity; it leads to normative feelings and the moral life by intermediaries which we examine later.

FOURTH STAGE: INTUITIVE AFFECTS AND THE BEGINNING OF INTERPERSONAL FEELINGS

The second major developmental period, which begins around two years with the appearance of language and representation, like the preverbal period, has three stages. From the cognitive point of view, this is the period of verbal or socialized intelligence; and from the affective point of view, it is the period of interpersonal or social feelings.

The appearance of the symbolic function brings about a fundamental transformation in the child's psychological life. Thanks to it, the child becomes able to evoke absent situations by means of arbitrary signifiers. Symbolic play, to which we shall have occasion to return at the end of the course, becomes superimposed on exercise play. Along with internalized representations in the form of mental images and language, it provides signifiers that make indefinite extension of intelligent adaptation possible by freeing the intellect from immediate perception. Intelligence comes to bear on the past as well as on the future, on distant space as well as near. At the same time, language allows thought to be socialized.

From the affective point of view, parallel transformations are seen. Representation and language allow feelings to acquire a stability and duration they have not had before. Affects, by being represented, last beyond the presence of the object that excites them. This ability to conserve feelings makes interpersonal and moral feelings possible and allows the latter to be organized into normative scales of values.

Let us begin by studying the simplest form of interpersonal feelings, i.e. liking and disliking others. Janet explained these feelings by extending his interpretation of internal regulations to the interpersonal plane. Just as feelings of being pressured or unpressured were involved in intra-individual actions, so, Janet believed, there were "fatiguing" individuals with whom interacting required effort and who were disliked and there were "economic" individuals who stimulated others and who were liked. Feelings of liking and disliking were, in Janet's view, nothing other than an interpersonal regulation of forces. It should be added that Janet's analysis was not a simple verbal generalization but was based on observations of psychasthenic behavior.

We have already indicated that we do not believe every aspect of behavior can be explained by its internal economy. Even in the preceding stage, recourse to the notion of valuation was necessary. With the present one, Janet's explanation appears to us to be still more unsatisfactory. While Janet's account may have some value as far as superficial and incidental likes and dislikes of other people are concerned, in the stage currently being discussed, such feelings are already more lasting and less tied to immediate action than Janet supposed they were. For this reason, another explanation must be found.

We might begin by asking ourselves whether liking someone could be reduced to mutual enrichment of the sort found in the classical utilitarian thesis of philosophers like John Stuart Mill. According to this doctrine, selfishness could lead to protecting other peoples' interests through an extension of self-interest. Altruism arose, therefore, only as an extension of the self. The utilitarian thesis rested on two postulates that need to be examined.

The first of these postulates was that all behavior was based on interest. The problem with this formula is that it is based on a double meaning of the word interest. In as much as interest designates something that activates behavior, it is an energetic term to which selfish or altruistic meaning, the other definition, cannot be attributed. Under the activation definition, interest stands in opposition to disinterest, not disinterestedness. If all behavior involves interest in the sense of activation, that does not mean that all behavior involves interest in the sense of selfishness. In fact, the selfish or unselfish character of activation interest cannot be judged in advance. A person might be interested (first sense) in performing a disinterested act, etc.

The second utilitarian postulate was that selfish behavior preceded altruistic behavior developmentally. This postulate was a matter of course for a certain psychology that held a priori that consciousness of the self was primitive. We know that this is not the case, however, and that the self is not differentiated from others at the beginning. For this reason, the term "egocentrism," by which we have designated this lack of differentiation, has a meaning opposite to selfishness. We also know that starting from this initial state, consciousness of the self and consciousness of others are correlatively constructed. To wonder whether selfishness precedes altruism or vice versa is to pose a false problem. The question is to understand how these two poles are simultaneously created.

These considerations lead us to see liking other people not so much as the consequence of the enrichment that each partner draws from the other but as a reciprocity of attitudes and values. In order to make the nature of the exchanges that occur when two individuals confront one another clear, consider Figure 1.

This figure indicates that Subject 1, by his acts, words, etc, exerts an action on Subject 2. This action (R_1) represents a negative expenditure for Subject 1 which will be appreciated by Subject 2. The satisfaction (S_2) that Subject 2 feels will, therefore, correspond to R_1. The roles, of course, can be reversed.

Up to now, we have been dealing with real or actual values corresponding to perceptual affects. On the representative level, however, virtual or potential values will be added to actual ones. Why this is so may be understood by recalling that sensorimotor exchanges were not remembered in any way. Feelings disappeared just as sensations did. In contrast to this, after representation becomes possible, feelings last in the sense that they can be recreated. Affective acknowledgement analogous to intellectual representation appears. This allows more than a lacuna or need to persist although it does not yet constitute a normative feeling and does not yet involve total reciprocity. Affective acknowledgment does, however, introduce a reciprocity of attitudes oriented in the direction of conservation. Subject 2, for example, will feel a debt (T_2) with respect to Subject 1. Because of reciprocity, he will invest Subject 1 with a positive value (V_1) manifested as a feeling of goodwill. If Subject 2 represented a social group instead on an individual, Subject 1 would acquire social credit, prestige, or reputation in the same circumstances. Again, this would be because of reciprocity.

Subject 1   Subject 2

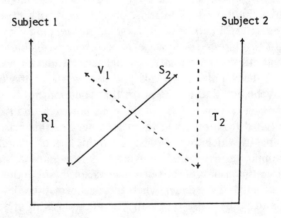

Figure 1 Diagram of interpersonal exchanges

The sociologist, Westermarck, investigated the elementary feelings leading to moral feeling, and his findings support what we are saying. In *Origine des idées morales*, Westermarck came to the conclusion that moral feelings originate from feelings of goodwill toward individuals who have given pleasure.

Positive interpersonal feelings presuppose, of course, that the partners' hierarchies of values are comparable and exchanges equal. There are, however, affective exchanges that are not equal. A person can give more than he receives or even give without receiving. Conversely, usury of virtual values or ingratitude may occur. In any case, such enrichment or devaluation as these exchanges may occasion is always a matter of reciprocal attitudes.

From all this, it is apparent how the ability to conserve and recreate experience provided by representation leads to the beginning of normative feelings. It is also obvious how analogous these feelings are to intellectual regulations.

Self-Estimation and Feelings of Superiority and Inferiority

There is estimation or evaluation of the self and, therefore, positive or negative self-esteem from the moment that a person begins to judge himself superior or inferior to other people. This in some ways replicates the schema of interpersonal attraction discussed previously. The importance of such feelings in the fourth stage and thereafter stems from the fact that they last beyond the circumstances giving rise to them and become permanent feelings of inferiority or superiority. It is important, therefore, to study their origin and construction.

The notion of *feelings of inferiority* was introduced by Adler who granted it a central role in his psychoanalytic system, and the idea has since become popular. Adler, as is well known, did not consider libido to be the fundamental instinct but accorded that honor to the *will to power*, to the drive to assert the ego. At its height this feeling, according to Adler, became the desire to dominate. The will to power encountered two obstacles during infancy, i.e. the adult world and organic inadequacies like physical malformations, sensory deficits, speech difficulties, etc. Inferiority feelings arose when the will to power was defeated. Adler also posited a compensatory or even overcompensatory drive. He held that the source of inferiority became the focus of the subject's interest and that overcompensation for it could, in certain cases, determine his vocation. To illustrate his point, Adler cited examples such as the fact that Demosthenes and Camille Desmoulins both had speech difficulties in childhood.

Claparède, too, spoke of a domination drive and linked it to a growth drive from which he believed it developed genetically. In addition, he distinguished four attitudes in the face of inferiority: (a) heroic compensation, for example the orator who stammers; (b) protective compensation, for example the child who whistles to conceal his fear; (c) fictitious compensations like play, dreams, art (cf Freudian sublimation); and (d) acceptance, often accompanied by exaggeration of the inferiority so as to make it an excuse for one's failures. All of these are acceptable in as much as they describe real facts; but, to our way of thinking, the whole problem of where inferiority and superiority feelings come from remains unsolved because neither Adler nor Claparède explains how values are established. We must attempt to do this and to understand the relationship of self-esteem to the hierarchy of values we discussed previously.

A first explanation we might consider would be that of the psychoanalyst, Odier. Odier did not accept Adler's explanation either. For him, feelings of inferiority resulted simply from lack of love or some other kind of affective frustration in childhood, and feelings of superiority resulted from an excess in the opposite direction. This interpretation seems inadequate to us, however, as does the Freudian monism generally. Love, as we have shown, is not solely an affective charge that creates different feelings by successive shifts of cathexis. Love presupposes a series of exchanges between individuals and involves evaluations that one cannot derive directly from the libido. Moreover, social successes and failures, which we have said elsewhere play an important role in the development of self-esteem, must also be taken into consideration in the genesis of inferiority feelings.

Shall we say, then, as has sometimes been said, that inferiority and superiority feelings are simply the result of other people's judgments, the subject devaluing himself to the degree that he is devalued by others and vice versa? Matters, it seems, are not so simple. Certainly, another person's attitude can influence the value one places on oneself. If a person is devalued by another person, three alternatives are open to him. He might, first of all, fail to take the judgment into account, but such an attitude is difficult to maintain. There is general agreement that the need for approval is one of man's profoundest needs. The sociologist, V. Pareto, even saw it as the foundation of human and societal relations. A second alternative would be to devalue the persons who are doing the judging as, for example, misunderstood artists are wont to do. This requires, however, the existence of a minority who approve of the person judged and from whom he draws support. The final alternative would be to accept the other person's judgment and to devalue oneself accordingly.

The fact that social influences affect the value a person places on himself does not mean that such influences are sufficient to account for every aspect of self-estimation, however. We have already seen on the sensorimotor level how, prior to social relationships properly so-called, success and failure can influence subsequent behavior, and we shall further see that from the fourth

stage onward the child evaluates himself continuously and often indepen-
dently of social relationships. Instead of a purely social origin, therefore, it
seems that we must invoke some application of socially acquired behavior
to the self. That this occurs is a law stated by Royce and also found in
Baldwin, G. Tarde, Janet, etc.[14] With regard to self-esteem, application of
social behavior to the self may be illustrated by the fact that people can have
a better or worse opinion of themselves than someone else does. Obviously,
they are evaluating themselves in some way and not just accepting the
evaluations of others. Our idea of what they are doing can best be understood by returning to the figure previously employed (Figure 1). It must be
understood, however, that Subjects 1 and 2 will in this case represent
processes internal to a single subject. The satisfaction that the subject feels
(S_2) in this case corresponds to his own action (R_1). He conserves the
"debt" (T_2) in the form of an enduring obligation toward himself as a
person, and the feeling of superiority or inferiority (V_1) is a function of
T_2.

In order to consider self-esteem from the point of view of economic and
qualitative values, we need to recall certain distinctions made earlier. We
said before that the regulation of action involves two systems. There are
energetic regulations, which are purely quantitative and correspond to the
internal economy of action. There is also an evaluation of one's action or
its effects, which is a qualitative system. The distinction between economic
and qualitative values is not the same as the distinction between action
proper and social behavior, however. Even in action proper, qualitative
values come into play alongside energetic regulations. Some positive or
negative quality is assigned to a person's action at the same time that
energies are calculated according to the principle of least effort. Social
exchanges, likewise, can involve either qualitative or economic values, and
the two types of exchange can be distinguished from the moment some
system of measurement is possible. This difference might be illustrated by
comparing the sorts of values involved when a mathematician and a psychologist exchange information during a conversation with the sorts of
values involved when a one-hour psychology lesson is exchanged for a
one-hour lesson in mathematics.

The Beginning of Moral Feelings

The next topic to be considered is the development of moral feelings. We
first look at the feelings involved in family interactions and then define
affective schemes by examining the problems of transference and the genesis
of the superego. Finally, after having analyzed moral sentiments like respect
and obedience, we introduce the idea of seminormative feelings.

[14]Cf autoimitation, internal language, etc. Janet sees reflection as the application of the
conversation schema to oneself.

In approaching the topic of affective schemes, we begin with the now classic Freudian solution to the problem of how the conscience is formed. This has to do, of course, with the genesis of the superego and introjection of parental authority. For Freud, moral feelings were derived from affects occurring within the family. He invoked fixations, identifications, and transferences to explain their formation and transformations. Although we have already seen the difficulties and inadequacies of this interpretation with respect to certain other topics, we examine it again with regard to interpersonal schemes of behavior and the formation of the superego.

Freud insisted at great length on the fact that affectivity was very early centered on the mother and father and involved feelings that energized verbal exchanges and other social behaviors (e.g. Oedipal complex). He used the term transference to designate the application of affective modalities relative to the father or mother to other people. According to Freud, therefore, the child entering school reacted to the new situation not only as a function of his own and his teacher's characters, but also as a function of his parents' personalities. In other words, the child's attitude, positive or negative with respect to his family, was transferred to the academic situation. Since transference is constantly at work, attitudes towards one's father and mother influenced a person's entire life.

Freud's explanation of the mechanism of transference rested on his conviction that affectivity was derived from a psychic energy that could be displaced from one situation to another or from a previous object or idea to a subsequent one. Unconscious fixation of psychic energy on representations of past events accounted for persistence of feelings about the parents. Identification of the mother or father with some person in the present accounted for the transference of these stored up feelings onto the latter.

While we do not disagree with Freud either about the existence of transference phenomena or about the fact that there is some way in which feelings are conserved, we suggest an alternative to his hypothesis about how affective conservation is effected. The Freudian hypothesis assumes that *feeling is conserved as such* and that this accounts for the obvious continuity of affective life from childhood to adulthood. According to this idea, the same feeling, e.g. agressivity, can be present, then disappear, then reappear. In other words, feeling passes from consciousness to unconsciousness and vice versa without ever being got rid of. An alternative possibility would be to assume that feelings are *reconstructed*. This hypothesis is similar to the one we defended with respect to object choice, and it is the one we shall champion here. In our view, it is not feeling that is conserved but a certain scheme of interaction with other people. Feeling, properly speaking, appears, disappears, and oscillates in intensity not because it sinks into or emerges from the unconscious but because it is created, then dissipates, then is recreated. In other words, it is constructed or reconstructed on each occasion.

With these alternative hypotheses in mind, let us turn to the idea of affective schemes and consider it in detail. By this term we do not mean that there exist schemes of affectivity in the same way that there exist cognitive schemes. To say that would either reintroduce the dichotomy between affectivity and intelligence that we have constantly denied, or it would inappropriately broaden the idea of scheme. Actually, there are not two kinds of schemes, cognitive and affective. There are, rather, schemes that have to do with people and schemes that have to do with objects. Both are cognitive and affective at the same time.

We have characterized schemes having to do with objects as modes of reaction that can be repeated and that, even more importantly, can be generalized. Even perceptual or sensorimotor schemes have these qualities. Not only are they patterns of reaction; they are also true instruments of generalization. Sucking, for instance, is soon applied to almost any object. When it is a matter of conceptual schemes such as the classifications seen in concrete logic, the generality is much greater. In effect, classification schemes apply to any object having certain properties in common with other members of a class. And in between schemes of motor action and conceptual schemes, a whole gamut of pre-conceptual schemes are found which are intermediary between the individual and the generic.

We hold that it is the same with schemes of reaction having to do with people. Our hypothesis is that interpersonal schemes make the subject react to people in more or less constant fashion in analogous situations even though the persons he is interacting with may vary. Schemes of this sort have their beginnings in the child's reactions to his parents, and the schematization of the individual's affective and cognitive reactions make up his character. Naturally, the formation of interpersonal schemes would be susceptible to energetic effects analogous to those studied on the intellectual plane.

This hypothesis appears more acceptable to us than the hypothesis of an unconscious reservoir of feelings. We note in this respect that some psychoanalysts after Freud have modified the theory of the unconscious and admit, at least implicitly, notions analogous to that of schemes. Nevertheless, identifications and condensations in the Freudian sense of those terms are found in manifestations of symbolic thought like dreams and symbolic play, and they are more direct than in the reconstructionist hypothesis just stated. It is, however, precisely in the area of imagery that these identifications, condensations, etc, are evident. This is an area where reconstruction does not come into play at all or comes into play in a minor way. In effect, dreams and symbolic play cannot be expressed by any means other than images where little schematization is involved.[15]

The prototype of interpersonal reaction schemes is what Freud called the *superego*. He viewed the superego as an internalization of the parents' personalities resulting in censorship, repression, and self-punishment. We disagree with this because, in our opinion, the superego cannot be reduced to parental images alone. It is, instead, a scheme that reproduces and, therefore, generalizes reactions to situations experienced in the past. In effect, what a person experiences and what he does at any moment in his life is a product of continuously assimilating current situations to situations experienced in childhood and vice versa. The superego is, therefore, a "reaction scheme" and not a reservoir of memories.

We propose, then, to explain the development of moral feelings as a particular instance of the construction of affective schemes. As it happens, the origin and development of the first moral feelings have given rise to all sorts of psychological studies, notably on the part of psychoanalysts. Let us review some of these with regard to the feelings of obedience and respect.

OBEDIENCE AND RESPECT   Even before Freud formulated his theory of the superego, Ferenczi wondered, in an article in *Imago,* why children obeyed their parents. He remarked that children did not obey just anyone and saw obedience as an internalization of parental orders which he thought could be explained by the special affective relationship that existed between children and their parents. According to Ferenczi, this relationship was made up of a mixture of affection and fear; but, in our view, neither affection nor fear can account for obedience. Surely something more than these two feelings is involved.

Baldwin also sought the origin of moral feelings in interpersonal relationships, but he did so in a way different from Ferenczi. For Baldwin, consciousness of the self originated from consciousness of the similarity, expressed and magnified by imitation, between others' and one's own gestures. In so far as the child also discovered his parents' selves through

[15]This paragraph is extremely obscure. It alludes to issues Piaget has discussed more fully in *Play, Dreams, and Imitation in Childhood* and which he later investigated extensively (*Mental Imagery in the Child* and *The Grasp of Consciousness*). The point is not that reconstruction plays no part in imagery (there are, in fact, reconstructive images) but that accurate reconstruction and, therefore, accurate imagery are impossible in dreams or symbolic play since accommodation is impeded. In Piaget's later writing on this subject, it is this lack of accommodation that produces the distortions Freud called condensation and displacement (here referred to as identification) and not Freud's mechanism of censorship and disguisement. For this reason, the facts of condensation and identification do not speak against Piaget's hypothesis of reconstruction.—Translators

imitation, interpersonal relationships resulted in the constitution of an "ideal self" which went beyond the child's individual self. This ideal self presented the same characteristics as the Freudian superego; and, according to Baldwin, it explained obedience. Here again, we do not believe the explanation given will prove adequate. No doubt Baldwin was correct in maintaining that obedience evolves from the child's acceptance of a submissive role, but his theory does not account for the feeling of obligation that is involved.

Pierre Bovet made a special search for the source of obligation (*Archives de Psychologie*, 1908, 1912). The originality and interest of Bovet's thesis lay in his defining this feeling not just in terms of the subject but also in terms of an *interpersonal relationship*. For Bovet, obligation had its origin in such a relationship, as it did for Baldwin; and, in addition, it constantly implied an interpersonal dimension. Two conditions were considered by Bovet to be necessary and sufficient for this feeling. First, one partner had to give *instructions* or orders of indefinite expiration which were valid in every situation and which were permanent, at least in so far as no countermanding order was given. Bovet offered as an example the instruction not to lie. The second condition was that the order be accepted. It was only under these contingencies that the special feeling in which fear and affection were mixed and which Bovet called *respect* made its appearance.

Certainly, the notion of respect is not new. All moralists have stressed its importance, but they have not seen it as a precocious interpersonal feeling. Kant, for example, did not consider respect a feeling like other feelings. He believed respect was not directed toward people but toward moral law as such. To respect another person was to respect the moral law he represented. Durkheim was Kantian and often busied himself transcribing Kant's ideas into "sociological" language by replacing the transcendental with the "collective conscience." For him, respect was respect for the "collective will." In any case, both Kant and Durkheim made respect the consequence of moral law. Bovet rejected these interpretations as genetically unacceptable. The child, he said, acquired respect for law only through respect for other people and not the reverse. Respect for other people was not the consequence, therefore, but the preliminary condition of moral law.

Bovet examined and criticized several classical hypotheses with regard to other factors that had been invoked to explain the formation of moral feelings. The first such factor, often invoked by sociologists, was habit. Habit engendered feelings that resembled moral feelings by introducing into behavior regularities and constraints similar to those of moral obligation. Bovet had no trouble responding to this contention that "good habits" were not developed automatically. If one considered their origin, one discovered that they were acquired through education, through example, or in other words, through interpersonal relationships in every case. Nor could "duty" be reduced to a sum of habits which, as such, did not engender obligation. In this regard, Baldwin remarked that duty was a sort of habit but one whose principal effect was to make us struggle against our habits!

Obvious decisions or resolutions had also been invoked as the source of moral feelings. Bovet observed subjects who gave themselves orders and suffered when they did not follow them. He saw this as only another example of socially acquired behavior applied to oneself, however, and contended that such decisions or resolutions were replications of interpersonal schemas.

Imitation, another of the factors that had been thought to be involved in the development of moral feelings, played an incontestable role according to Bovet; but he thought that invoking it only displaced the problem. The motives behind imitation still had to be understood. The child did not imitate just anyone; he imitated only those adults, elders, or contemporaries whom he considered superior to himself. Imitation could consolidate the feeling of obligation or facilitate obedient behavior; but, with the child as well as with the adult, imitation presupposed obligation and could not explain it.

Social constraint was the last factor Bovet considered. It had long been a recurrent theme of sociologists in discussions of moral feeling. For Durkheim, an imperative was obligatory because it was collective. If the child obeyed his father, it was because the latter possessed and represented social authority. Bovet responded that it was very improbable that a child 18 to 24 months old recognized the collective will in his father. Moreover, children had no difficulty accepting rules imposed but not followed by adults. Such rules could not have had an absolute or collective character in the Durkheimian sense. If a father forbade a child to touch his papers, this rule had the same coercive and obligatory character for the child as the rule not to lie which his parents, themselves, adhered to. In general, it was difficult, according to Bovet, to maintain that the father was obeyed because he embodied a moral tradition of the social group when the two year old child in no way discerned the group or its representatives.

Let us adopt Bovet's criticisms and his hypothesis that the feeling of obligation is tied to the interpersonal feeling of respect. This hypothesis, by itself, does not prove sufficient to explain the entire evolution of moral feelings, however. It is only applicable to the heteronomous morality of obedience. That other sorts of morality exist is suggested by the care Bovet takes to distinguish between the feeling of "duty" and the feeling of "moral righteousness" which develops later. In order to take these other levels into account Bovet's theory must be made more specific and must be corrected on certain points. To this end, we introduce the idea of seminormative feelings.

SEMINORMATIVE FEELINGS   Bovet's description is a description of *unilateral respect* which characterizes the morality of obedience. This is the first feeling that heralds *normative feelings;* or in other words, it is the first feeling that has to do with what it is necessary and not just what it is desirable or preferable to do. Normative feelings, properly speaking, appear only during the following stage in the form of autonomous morality and mutual respect. We can glimpse the beginning of the transition during this stage, however, and can describe it using the term *seminormative feelings* just as we used the term preoperational representations to describe the parallel transition evident on the cognitive plane.

Recall that in studying the development of intelligence, we characterized the preoperational level by reasoning involving rudimentary forms of operations still linked to perceptual configurations. An example of such operations is the bi-univocal correspondence of two collections. During the fourth stage, the child concluded that two collections of counters, red and blue, are numerically equal by placing their elements in one-to-one correspondence. If, however, the perceptual configuration is modified by shortening or lengthening one of the collections without removing any counters, the child no longer believes that both collections contain equal numbers of elements. A second example is the child's notion of speed. This appears quite early and arises from the child's observation of moving objects. A first object is faster for the child than a second object if he sees the first object pass the second. If, however, the child is shown two objects moving at different speeds which enter and exit from tunnels of unequal length at the same time, he will say that the two speeds are equal since he did not see one pass the other. If the two tunnels are removed so that the child can see the trajectories, he will give the correct response. Data of this sort indicates quite clearly that preoperational thought remains bound to perceptual experience.

As far as feelings are concerned, analogous phenomena are found on the preoperational level. Feelings are not yet normative, but they prepare the way for the establishment of moral norms defined by three characteristics parallel to the criteria for operations: (a) a moral norm is generalizable to all analogous situations, not just to identical ones; (b) a moral norm lasts beyond the situation and conditions that engender it; and (c) a moral norm is linked to a feeling of autonomy.

From two to seven years, none of these conditions is met. To begin with, norms are not generalized but are valid only under particular conditions. For example, the child considers it wrong to lie to his parents and other grown-ups but not to his comrades. After the age of eight, however, children understand that it is wrong to lie in any situation, and they even argue in a valid way that lying to one's comrades is more serious. Second, instructions remain linked to certain represented situations analogous to perceptual configurations. An instruction, for example, will remain linked to the person who gave it, or children will judge that a lie is "not as naughty" if the person duped is unaware he has been lied to ("moral realism"). Finally, there is no autonomy during the preoperational period. "Good" and "bad" are defined as that which conforms or fails to conform to the instructions one has received.

This is why we speak only of seminormative feelings. Such feelings represent a particular case of the interpersonal exchange relationships diagrammed in Figure 1. In this case, Subject 1 represents an authority who gives orders or instructions, and Subject 2 represents the person who receives the order. R_1 is the authority's act of giving the instruction. S_2 signifies a sui generis satisfaction that Subject 2 takes in being asked to do something for Subject 1. This is accompanied by respect, in Bovet's sense, which is felt for the person who gives the order. T_2 is a debt felt by Subject 2 as an obligation to obey. This arises as a function of R_1 and S_2. Finally V_1 takes on the meaning of a moral value.

In effect, this sort of internalized exchange is the basis of *moral realism*. In this sort of morality, the norm or order, although internalized, is experienced as being external to the individual, or in other words, as existing in itself. An example of this would be a little girl who is made to drink a cup of chocolate every day even though she does not like it. She protests against this obligation but complies. Then one day when the constraint is dispensed with in order to please her, she protests against the dispensation and refuses to take advantage of it.

Moral realism is also particularly obvious in the objective conception of responsibility. Different forms of responsibility are defined in terms of what is to be penalized. In the case of objective responsibility, the seriousness of a transgression is a function of the material results of an action and not of the agent's intention. Subjective responsibility, on the other hand, refers to the intention only. The sociologists Westermarck and Fauconnet found that some primitive societies conceive responsibility objectively. With social evolution, responsibility is internalized at the same time that the moral agent becomes autonomous. This gives rise to the subjective morality of intention. Without prejudging whether there is any onto-phylogenetic parallelism, the analogy between individual and social evolution should be indicated, and it should be stressed that the transition from moral realism to autonomous morality is easily observed in children.

A good example of this is furnished by the study of how children recognize and evaluate *lies*. First, it is necessary to distinguish lies, properly so-called, from what Stern calls "pseudo-lies." In the latter, the subject, himself, is duped. It is also necessary to distinguish lies from symbolic play where the child assimilates reality to his momentary interests and falls into playful fantasies which distort reality. Neither pseudo-lies nor these voluntary fictions of imaginary play nor situations where children accuse themselves of mistakes they have not made are really lying. Lying, properly so-called, takes on meaning for the child only with the development of social life. At the stage under consideration, it cannot be clearly perceived or appreciated.

The technique for studying lies consists in asking the child for the definition of lying and then having him compare stories, one containing an intention to deceive and another a simple exaggeration. The child must repeat the stories, explain the motivations of the characters, judge whether the stories are lies, and give his reasons. "If you were a Papa," he is asked, "would you find these two lies equally bad?" In this way three facts are observed. First, the child fails to distinguish truth from accuracy or to differentiate lies from what must not be said. "Two plus two equals five" and "naughty words" are both lies for the child because "this is not true" or "it is bad to say that." Second, examples of lying provided by the child indicate poorly whether there is an intention to deceive; malicious lies and defensive lies are put in the same category as bluffs. Finally, in comparing stories, the seriousness of a lie is made a function of its material content and not of the intention behind it.

As an example, consider the following stories:

Story 1. Returning from school, a young boy tells his mother that he was quizzed and received a good mark when nothing of the sort had happened. His mother rewards him with some chocolate.

Story 2. A little boy meets a large dog on his way home from school. When he gets home, he tells his mother he saw a dog as big as a cow.

Around seven or eight years of age, children immediately make a suitable differentiation between stories like these. From two to seven years of age, however, they generally think that the second one is more serious than the first. This is so, they say, "because no one ever saw a dog like that" but "it could happen" that the boy got a good mark. Or they justify their answers by saying that the mother would have seen immediately that the second story was a lie, while in the first case she could not have known. It is apparent, therefore, that for the child a statement is more deceitful the more its content is unlikely. Analogous investigations were carried out by Caruso in Louvain who found responses different from those cited here but with a marked distinction between two types of answers given.

Another example is found in the child's reaction to punishment. The technique employed was the same as the one above, i.e. two stories were compared. Small children feel punishment to be necessary and just, and moral realism leads them to make an exact balance between misdeeds and punishments or even between punishments and injuries. Here, too, examples may be used to ask whether, the culprit being unknown, it would be better to punish everyone or not to punish anyone for fear of punishing the innocent. Children six to eight give delicately shaded responses but prefer not to punish anyone. By contrast, younger children call for collective punishment since there has been a misdeed and since in their eyes no misdeed can go unpunished. Also, they characteristically believe in immanent punishment. For example, the following story and question are presented:

> A child touches some scissors that his mother had forbidden him to touch; a little later he takes a walk and crosses a stream on a plank; suddenly, the plank gives way and he falls in the stream. Why did he fall?

Older children will respond without hesitation that he fell because the plank was rotten and that the two parts of the story are unrelated. Younger children, on the contrary, connect the two parts and resist any suggestion to the contrary.

> "Why did he fall?"
> "Because he disobeyed."
> "And if he had not disobeyed?"
> "He would still have fallen."
> "Then why did he fall?"
> "Because he disobeyed." Etc.

FIFTH STAGE: NORMATIVE AFFECTS

The fifth stage begins around seven or eight and lasts until the child is eleven or twelve years old. Let us first review its characteristics from the cognitive perspective. Since this stage is one of operations, properly speaking, the discussion will require that we have the definition of operations in mind.

An operation is an internalized system of actions that is fully reversible. Reversibility is made possible by the fact that the actions in the system are arranged in inverse pairs. In other words, for every action in the system there is another action that reverses it, and the two actions performed in succession arrive back at the starting point. For systems of this sort to exist, it is necessary that the elements on which they act be invariant. Concepts, relations, etc, cannot change from one moment to the next; or in the case of "cooperation," they must not vary from one person to another. Reversibility of their transformations and invariance of their elements insures that operational systems or "structures" will be conserved as totalities throughout their functioning. This indicates the importance of "conservation" as an index of mental operations. Examples of operational systems that appear on the concrete level are classification or seriation structures.

The question is whether similar structures exist in the affective domain. In this respect, we have already suggested that the development of feelings tends toward equilibrium. Values are initially linked to what is happening at a given moment. By the fourth stage, however, they have begun to be conserved. In the stage currently under discussion and in the subsequent stage they will be progressively coordinated and will, as moral feelings or normative affects, come to constitute reversible systems parallel to operational systems of intelligence. We shall successively examine the conservation of feelings, the problem of the will, which introduces a certain form of reversibility into affective life, and, finally, the autonomous moral feelings such as justice and mutual respect belonging to this stage.

Conservation of values, as we shall see, implies a logic of feelings. At the same time, this term seems paradoxical. On the one hand, we refuse to use this term, as Ribot did, to label the illogicality of impassioned reasoning. This is because, in our opinion, affectivity only makes rational thought deviate into all sorts of paralogisms; it does not form coherent systems as is the case with reason. On the other hand, however, we cannot agree with the alternative position that "logic of feelings" is a contradiction in terms. That contention is based on the premise that the terms used in an argument must be invariable so that they may be compared while feelings are variable and cannot be compared to one another without changing them. While this may be true when only intra-individual and spontaneous interpersonal feelings are considered, it is no longer true when feelings begin to be conserved. If there can be no logic of feelings so long as feelings do not last from one situation to another, that does not mean that a logic of feelings cannot exist at all. As it happens, social life requires thought to acquire a certain permanence. For this to occur, mental activity can no longer be represented in terms of personal symbols such as playful fantasies but will have to be expressed in universal signifiers such as linguistic signs. The uniformity and consistency of expression enforced by social life plays a large part, therefore, in the development of intellectual structures with their conservations and invariants; and it will lead to analogous transformations in the domain of feelings. In effect, the permanence obviously lacking from spontaneous feelings will appear with social and, especially, with moral feelings.

Many examples of this can be found. For instance, liking another person is a feeling that varies as long as it is spontaneous and linked to particular situations. It becomes lasting and reliable when feelings of semi-obligation are added. We have already described the origin and mechanism of this transformation in the discussion of values. Likes or dislikes of other people will become even more durable with acts of will; and gratitude, a fragile feeling in the young child, will be stabilized by the conservation of values and autonomous moral obligation. Truthfulness, also, and the feeling of justice will come to form stable and coherent systems as the child develops. We contend, therefore, that any true logic of affectivity must be sought in feelings of this sort. It is not present in the intuitive affects but makes its appearance in the feelings that develop out of them. Affective logic does not, however, consist purely and simply in the imposition of intellectual logic on intuitive affects, as we shall see later.

Despite every analogy, some people will say that moral feelings, however normative they may be, remain less universal, less stable, and less coercive than operational rules. This objection, in our opinion, is unfounded. If, in fact, some difference between logical and moral norms were to be found, it would be one of degree not one of nature. On the whole, we believe this difference to be weaker than is ordinarily imagined. Common thought is at least as far removed from operational norms as everyday behavior is from moral norms.

The Problem of the Will

The affective analogue of intellectual operations is found in the act of will. The will is an instrument for conserving values and is one of the affective characteristics of the fifth stage. Some precautions of vocabulary are necessary, however, when discussing acts of will. In everyday language as well as in the language used by psychologists, the term, will, is given various meanings. It is important not to confuse them. When a young child shows any evidence of energy, people usually say he has "a will of his own" even though he is only pursuing his whims. Similarly, voluntary movement as opposed to reflexive movement is unrelated to the will as we use the term. Many behaviors that could be qualified as volitional in one way or another appear before and after our fifth stage. We, however, are interested only in behaviors that are characteristic of normative affects. Taking inspiration from William James, we define such behavior by two criteria. First, in order to speak of will, a conflict between two impulses or tendencies must be present. Second, the impulse that is initially weaker must become the stronger of the two in the course of an act of will. This means that all hypotheses concerning the will must account for this reversal.

Philosophers, sociologists, and psychologists have proposed many models to explain the will. Let us begin our brief review of the principal varieties of these models by considering the affective theories of the will. In the manner of Condillac, all such theories reduce the will to an exclusive or predominate impulse. There is deep-rooted confusion inherent in this idea, however, a confusion also found in Wundt for whom the will amounted to the conative element of every impulse. The will, said Wundt, is that in every affective state which tends to prolong the state when it is agreeable and to suppress it when it is not. The same definition was given by Ribot and a related one by Rignano for whom there was will whenever a remote intention prevailed over a current one. Such theories are, at best, descriptions. They leave untouched the problem of knowing how this predominance is realized. It is the same with theories that identify will with effort. One still must ask where this effort comes from and how it works.

Intellectual theories like that of Descartes situate the will in the analysis of judgment. The act of intelligence comprises two stages: conception which is the work of the understanding, and affirmation which is the work of the will. The Cartesian will was nothing other than the power to accept or to refuse what the understanding had conceived. In the final analysis, it was the freedom of the mind. Spinoza went still further by identifying understanding and will, the latter being only the force of our ideas. These philosophical theories are interesting for the psychologist because they indicate the analogy between logical and moral judgments; but that does not mean that moral judgment can be reduced to logical judgment. Intellectual theories, in fact, cannot explain the working of the will unless one concludes, as Descartes did, that the will decides in sovereign fashion, that it has absolute power, that it is infinite even as the will of God. The psychologist cannot be satisfied with this.

There are also several personality theories of the will. Warren and various gestaltists held that the act of will involved intervention of the entire personality whereas simpler acts, e.g. impulsive behaviors, were only partial behaviors of the self. It is difficult to see anything in this that makes the will a distinct entity or how such a conception could account for conflicts.

William James's description of acts of will is interesting and was followed in our previous definition. One could hardly say that it is an explanatory theory, however. James began with conflict and established that the force of the will was oriented in the direction of greatest resistance. It effected, therefore, a reversal in the relationship between the forces opposing one another. James did not succeed in explaining this reversal and even gave up trying to provide an explanation. He had to content himself with establishing that the phenomenon existed. Will, he said, is a "fiat." This mystical word shows that James was perfectly conscious of the limits of his explanation.

Binet, criticizing James (*Année Psychologique*, 1911), interpreted the reversal in the following way. If what was initially weak became strong in the end, it was necessary to assume some "additional force" had come into play. He reproached James for not explaining this. It is not certain that James wished to speak of a supplementary force, but other theorists have tried to take account of this energetic gain assumed by Binet.

Another interesting conception is the sociological theory of Charles Blondel. In *La psychologie collective* as well as in the article in Dumas' treatise, Blondel revived James's proposal and congratulated him for having known how to pose the problem clearly. According to Blondel, the supplementary force that reversed the relationship between impulses was, indeed, an energy of the person, but was of social origin. It came, so to speak, from internalization of the "collective imperative;" or, as Blondel put it, it was a "gift Society has put in our cradle." As such, it was much stronger than individual impulses. In addition, Blondel distinguished different reactions to social imperatives. There was the conformist reaction of the masses, "that great mob of men," as Péguy called it, "who wish through a ready-made will" and who simply follow the imperatives in favor with their social group. There were also nonconformist reactions. Blondel believed it was necessary to distinguish carefully between an unadapted anarchic variety where the individual was in conflict with the group not because his own will was strong but because, on the contrary, it was inadequate, and an élite variety where the individual was in conflict with the group because he better represented its aspirations than did the imperatives in force. The latter notion is identical with Durkheim's theory of great men.

Without passing judgment on the value this explanation may have for sociology, we must say that the psychologist cannot be content with it. Even if one were to agree that the "fiat" is a social effect, that still would not explain how the conflict of impulses is resolved. If the subject simply relies on the social imperative, one could hardly go on speaking of will. If this imperative is internalized, it then acts as a personal impulse. It might owe its origin to a greater force, but initially it would still be the weaker impulse in the conflict. Blondel's conception would not explain how the internalized social imperative takes precedence over other impulses during the contest of will.

Claparède's theory reformulated James's notion in psychological terms. Even though he may not have found a satisfactory solution, Claparède made important observations we need to consider. The act of will, as Claparède rightly said, is a readaptation in the case of conflicting impulses, just as the act of intelligence is a readaptation in the case of a momentary loss of adaptation. This important analogy puts us on the path to a solution. Claparède adopted James's model but specifically added that the impulse that triumphed in the volitional act was the "higher impulse." It is not clear, however, what this moral qualification of "higher" meant from the strictly psychological point of view. Even Claparède gave up trying to define it. As for the "additional force," Claparède suggested that it might be analogous to certain phenomena of a physiological order such as the acceleration of internal secretions. Let us retain Claparède's analogy between intellectual acts of readaptation and acts of will, but go on to describe and explain the will as a special behavioral regulation.

Will as Regulation of Regulations

If acts of will are compared to intellectual operations, it is obvious that it is no longer necessary to make an additional force intervene. In problems of intelligence one encounters conflicts between perceptual experience and logical deduction. The subject must rise above the momentary perceptual configuration. He must free himself from it in order to bring out relationships that were not given in perception at the start. This involves decentration, which permits mastery of the present situation by connecting it with former situations and, if need be, by anticipating future ones. That is how an operation works.

Our thesis here is that it is exactly the same with acts of will. Affective conditions are given which correspond to the perceptual configuration of intellectual operations. It is not a question of rejecting this affective configuration but of going beyond it by "changing perspective" in such a way that relationships appear that were not given at the start. There is nothing any more mysterious about this than about intellectual decentration. *The will is simply the affective analogue of intellectual decentration.* The force of the impulses in conflict is in no way absolute; in every case, it is relative to the configuration. The "change of perspective," by modifying the situation, modifies the distribution of constantly varying forces.

In our opinion, the traditional conception of the will in its antagonistic form falsifies the problem. It imagines a combat between two independent impulses, each having its own force. Such a conception is particularly hard pressed to explain the outcome of this conflict since the element that is initially the weakest triumphs in the end. We must no longer appeal to verbal explanations or substitute a moral justification for psychological explanation as Claparède did when he held that the impulse that was energetically weaker was morally better, etc. That is an evident sophism. The problem is that the antagonistic conception is untrue. The force of an impulse is not fixed, even if it is the only one in play. We have already seen this in our study of regulations, and it is even more true when two antagonistic impulses are apparent. The force of an impulse depends at every instant on the configuration of the affective field, just as in perceptual experience the comparative *prégnance* of the elements of the configuration depends on the perceptual field. The consecutive modification of forces which occurs in decentration is a field effect.

When adults introspect during acts of will, they have no trouble finding evidence of decentration with respect to an initial situation. Not just intellectual decentration is involved, however. Certainly, representations, judgments, etc, intervene in the course of the conflict. This is because there is no purely affective behavior nor any that is purely intellectual. But decisions of the will are not just products of reasoning or effects of representation. Decentration brings one's past to life again not just by connecting current situations with past ones or linking present perceptions with images from the past. It also recreates feelings and values momentarily forgotten. Since the expression "affective memory" has been contested, let us say that when a person recalls past situations, he relives values as well as memory images. One cannot reproach such an interpretation for being intellectualist or for explaining the will by intellectual operations. Decentration of values, while presupposing it, is parallel to and cannot be reduced to cognitive decentration.

The objection might still be made that we take the result for the cause. In order to decenter himself, it might be said, the subject must have a certain energy available, and that energy is the will. Our solution, if this were the case, would only have displaced the problem. This objection does not seem valid to us, however, because decentration does not require more energy than ordinary regulations and all regulations do not involve acts of will.

We end with this final formulation: the will is a regulation to the second power, a regulation of regulations, just as, from the cognitive point of view, the operation is an action on actions. The act of will corresponds, therefore, to the conservation of values; it consists of subordinating a given situation to a permanent scale of values.

Autonomous Feelings

In the fifth stage, new moral feelings are superimposed on preceding ones. We shall call these autonomous feelings. After seven or eight years of age, the child becomes capable of making his own moral evaluations, performs freely decided acts of will, and exhibits moral feelings which, in certain cases, conflict with the feelings seen in the heteronomous morality of obedience. The feeling of justice is completely characteristic of this latter sort of feeling. It indicates a new development in the area of moral feeling which will occasion significant conflicts with adults.

Also in this stage, feelings become organized into a system of relatively fixed values to which the child feels obliged to adhere. A new attitude, moral reciprocity, appears. This is normative and entails a sense of "duty." It is expressed in the feelings of mutual respect that appear during this stage. We shall show how this differs from unilateral respect in a fundamental way and how it becomes the origin of a profound enrichment of preexisting feelings.

The feeling of justice can be experimentally studied by observing the child's attitude with respect to the rules of childhood games. Lambercier and I (*The Moral Judgment of the Child,* Chapter 1) illustrated this using the game of marbles. The children we studied characteristically played this game in primary school and quit playing it in adolescence. We attempted to determine how they obeyed rules and what consciousness they had of them.

In Switzerland, the rules of marbles are very detailed and constitute a rigorous code. In our experiments, we systematically violated the rules while playing marbles with our subjects. Four attitudes could be discerned in their reactions. First, children who had never seen anyone else play, played an individual game without even making rules for themselves. They exhibited few regularities or habits, and even those they did employ had no normative character. Second, children who had seen older comrades play imitated them. They accepted older children's rules without discussion. However, because the rules were very complex, these children only knew them in part. Unilateral respect caused them to scrupulously apply those they had retained, but cooperation was not possible. In fact, from two to seven, each child played by himself even when playing with other children. A third attitude appeared around seven. This was when the rules were first completely known and observed. It was the first instance of really social play. Children who had achieved this level played according to common rules; there was a winner and a loser. Finally, around 12, children knew the whole code and manifested lively interest in it. They would write the rules down, etc.

The child's consciousness of rules and not just his obedience to them, conscious or unconscious, was examined by asking the child to invent a new rule, to say whether it was a "true rule," and also to say who had made the rules in force. Two attitudes stood out clearly.

On the egocentric level before seven years of age, true rules were the traditional ones. These were sacred and eternal; there was no question of changing them. True rules had been formulated once and for all by an authority, i.e. by the parents, by God who had put them into the parents' mind, by the government, etc. This attitude coincided with the heteronomous morality of obedience and unilateral respect. After seven years of age, children played according to the traditional code but accepted the idea that rules could be modified. Rules, the subjects said, "have been invented by kids my own age." They were, therefore, contingent on the common will. Certainly, children continued to respect rules scrupulously when they were playing, but unilateral and mystical respect was replaced by relative respect founded on reciprocity.

Interestingly enough, the same transformations are seen with regard to moral feelings. For example, the child in the fifth stage evaluates the seriousness of a lie as a function of the intention to deceive and evaluates misdeeds as a function of the subjective violation of rules instead of in terms of material damage. Starting at seven, children unanimously agree that distributive justice should be primary. This is evidence that autonomy is developing.

The notion of *autonomy* is employed here without philosophical import. It only means that it is possible for the subject to elaborate his own norms, at least in part. In his behavior, of course, he continues to apply rules that he did not invent and that were initially imposed on him by others; but the very way in which he employs them attests to his moral autonomy. His attitude with respect to the rules of games furnishes an example of this. It also illustrates François Rauh's contention that moral laws are general and that the way an individual applies them in particular situations, i.e. moral experience, is an authentic and constant creation.

In addition to the feeling of justice, the feeling of mutual respect may be used to exemplify autonomous feelings. In doing so, let us recall that Pierre Bovet wondered whether mutual respect could not be reduced to double unilateral respect. Genetic studies lead us to see something other than unilateral respect in reciprocal respect, however. Unilateral respect was present in the morality of obedience. It is the respect of the lower for the higher, for authority. Mutual respect differs from this in that it occurs between equals and appears only with autonomy. Certainly, until mutual respect in the strict sense appears, a foundation of unilateral respect constantly underlies adult-child relationships. In relationships among children, however, one observes all the intermediary nuances from attenuated unilateral respect toward older children to mutual respect. We must try to understand what constitutes the unique quality of mutual respect and what accounts for its autonomous character.

Durkheim believed that social pressure was the basis of mutual respect. For sociologists of his school, autonomy was nothing other than the internalization of the pressures of the "collective conscience." They did not explain the mechanism of this internalized pressure, however.

For our part, we believe that both continuity and heterogeneity exist between the two forms of respect just as continuity and heterogeneity with all possible transitions exist between asymmetrical and symmetrical relations in logic. In the affective domain, the characteristic of reciprocity appears to us to be the substitution of points of view. Let us again refer to the diagram (Figure 1) that was employed to explain exchanges. In mutual respect, four transformations are in operation.

1. Subject 1 acts by placing himself at Subject 2's point of view. R_1 is no longer just any action whatsoever of Subject 1 in the presence of Subject 2. It is an action Subject 1 performs for Subject 2.
2. The value S_2, which Subject 2 ascribes to R_1, is no longer only a function of the material satisfaction he draws from it. R_1 is not evaluated according to Subject 2's own scale of values. Its value is determined as a function of Subject 1's intention and according to Subject 1's scale of values.
3. The debt T_2 is felt by Subject 2 as obligatory gratitude.
4. The value V_1 attributed by Subject 2 to Subject 1 is no longer a simple affective value but is, instead, a moral value.

Let us consider in what way it might be said that reciprocity becomes obligatory. Here again, we can use an analogy to what transpires on the cognitive plane. Mutual respect entails the necessity of moral noncontradiction. One cannot simultaneously value his partner and act in such a way as to be devalued by him. At least that is the norm. Morality may in actual fact deviate from that norm just as common thought may deviate from the rules of logical noncontradiction.

In closing, we point out the criticism M. Davy made of the concept of mutual respect. In the chapter of Dumas' *Traité* devoted to "moral feelings," Davy objected that mutual respect was only a form of mutualism, an ordinary type of social behavior (cf the principle of an eye for an eye and a tooth for a tooth) from which moral feelings could not be derived directly. He further objected that autonomy was explained, as Durkheim had shown, by the internalization of social pressure.

We have already said what we thought of Durkheim's thesis. Social pressure is in no way sufficient to explain autonomy; and familial pressures, in particular, can be internalized without autonomy resulting. This problem is comparable to the one, previously illustrated, inherent in Freud's reduction of the superego to the introjection of parental authority. With regard to Davy's remarks about the reduction of mutual respect to mutualism, we need recall only that this respect is not just any reciprocity but precisely and specifically a reciprocity of points of view.

SIXTH STAGE: IDEALISTIC FEELINGS AND FORMATION OF THE PERSONALITY

The last stage of intellectual development is that of the formal operations. It begins around eleven or twelve and attains equilibrium around fourteen or fifteen. Let us briefly review the transformations observed at this level.[16]

It is during this stage that the capacity for hypothetico-deductive reasoning first appears. Henceforth, intelligence will be able to operate not only on objects and situations but also on hypotheses and, therefore, on the possible as well as on the real. This new form of reasoning will be evident in the adolescent's conversation as well as in his thinking about experimental problems.[17] Formal operations are not concerned only with operations on classes and relations as the concrete operations were. They operate on propositions and involve implication, disjunction, etc. They make it possible for the content of reasoning to be dissociated from its form. To simple operations bearing directly on objects or classes of objects, they add operations to the second power or operations on operations. This makes reflection in the strict sense possible; it allows thought to turn upon itself. In other words, formal operations make it possible for a person to think about what and how he thinks. In addition, these operations are combinatory.

Formal thought is indispensible for the integration of the adolescent into adult society. We remark in this respect a clear distinction between adolescence and puberty. The age of puberty varies much less according to climates and civilizations than has been claimed. The age at which the child

---

[16]For detailed studies, see Jean Piaget: "La période des opérations formelles et le passage de la logique de l'enfant à celle de l'adolescent," *Bulletin de Psychologie,* Vol. VII, No. 5 (February, 1954), p. 247.

[17]Cf B. Inhelder, "Les attitudes expérimentales de l'enfant et de l'adolescent," Ibid., p. 272.

ceases to feel he is a child and is integrated into the social body varies much more.

There are three characteristic aspects of this integration. First, the adolescent feels equal to adults. He tends either to imitate them in all respects or to contradict them. Second, the adolescent endeavors to integrate his work into social life. Up to this time, this had been a privilege only of adults. This integration will be professional if the adolescent devotes himself to effective work. If not, it will be a life-plan requiring a longer or shorter period for its realization. Finally, the adolescent tends to want to reform society in one way or another.

It is obvious that if the adolescent is to be able to envision the future and elaborate ideas that are not tied to the needs of the moment, he will have need of affective instruments, i.e. moral, social, and idealistic feelings, as well as intellectual ones. Let us begin by examining the interest for the social body which begins in adolescence.

As early as 11 or 12 years, cognitive and affective transformations in the direction of the formal operations are evident in the child's behavior. The first indications appear with the "juridical feelings" seen in play. Interest in rules and in the structure of the play group progressively increases. Children elaborate detailed statutes and conventions before proceeding to action. Adolescence is, in general, characterized by the elaboration of theories, systems, or doctrines. These are used to assimilate, and, where needed, to reform the ambiant ideology in every area, whether social, political, religious, metaphysical, or aesthetic. Concomitant changes occur in the affective domain. These can be labeled idealistic feelings. For us, these feelings define the personality. Up to 12 years of age, the child exhibits few feelings about ideas per se. His feelings are of a concrete sort directed toward objects or toward other people. Such values as he places on ideas are other people's values. These remain labile, since they are connected to the individual who represents them, and are quick to change or crumble. This is not to say that people do not retain great importance for the adolescent, but they do so because they mediate ideal values. They make it possible for the adolescent to relate to ideals and to participate progressively in the collective conscience through particular individuals. Examples of this will be found in our investigation of the idea of homeland which appeared in *Bulletin des Sciences Sociales de l'U.N.E.S.C.O.*[18]

Such is the intellectual and affective ambiance in which the personality is formed. Naturally, the term personality is taken here in its narrow sense.

---

[18]"Le développement chez l'enfant de l'idée de patrie et des relations avec l'étranger," *Bulletin International des Sciences Sociales,* Vol. III (1951), No. 3, pp. 605–50.

The personality is not identical with the self, and one could even say that it is oriented in the opposite direction. In effect, the self is activity that is centered on the self. The personality, on the other hand, develops at the time of entry into social life. Consequently, it presupposes decentration and subordination of the self to the collective ideal.

Charles Blondel usefully insisted on this distinction. He defined personality by the individual's social role, but he also included coenesthetic considerations in his definition. The latter, apparently, was done because of Ribot's influence. It is important to recall, therefore, that Ribot believed the basis of personal identity or the primitive form underlying the diverse manifestations of the permanent self to lie in consciousness of one's own body. He supported his analysis with pathological cases, strongly in vogue at the time, of "double personalities." In our view, coenesthesis[19] is a precognitive element from which one can derive neither the personality nor consciousness of the self directly.

Blondel started with Ribot's analysis and in *La conscience morbide* maintained that normal consciousness was, essentially, a socialized consciousness. He did not say that coenesthesis, which is not socializable, would be repressed. Rather, he said it would be "decanted." Coenesthesis, according to Blondel, continued to assure permanence of the self. He also believed that troubles with coenesthesis were manifested first in mental illness.

Later, in *La personnalité*, Blondel insisted on the social aspect exclusively. In this work, he maintained that the personality was, according to the expression of Ramon Fernandez, the mask or "persona" that one wore in society. Blondel ended this discussion by considering the problem of individual types. Strong personalities, he said, were those where collective ideals crystallize around individual temperament. From this point of view, coenesthesis took on a positive meaning. Far from escaping or opposing social influences, strong personalities created within the social system as they also did in Durkheim's theory of great men. Weak personalities modeled themselves on others.

Without going further into the detail of Blondel's theory, we shall retain from it the notion that personality in the strict sense can be defined neither

[19]Coenesthesis is defined by psychologists as the undifferentiated complex of organic sensation through which one becomes aware of his body. Ernst Heinrich Weber stressed the distinction between coenesthetic and sensory perception saying that coenesthesis referred to "one's ability to perceive his own general state of sensations (for example, pleasantness, unpleasantness, or nausea) as distinguished from the ability to have a sensation that he understands as an object different from his own sensory state." (Richard J. Herrnstein and Edwin G. Boring, *A Source Book in the History of Psychology*. Cambridge: Harvard University Press, 1965)—Translators

in terms of the self alone nor as the self. The "third year personality crisis" is very different from the personality crisis seen in adolescence. With the latter, it is not a matter, properly speaking, of progress in consciousness of the self. It is, rather, according to the definition given by I. Meyerson in *Les fonctions mentales et les oeuvres*, a matter of the fusion of one's work with one's individuality.

GENERAL CONCLUSIONS

These lectures have attempted to bring out the striking parallel that exists between the cognitive and affective aspects of behavior at every developmental level and have constantly underscored the relationship between intelligence and affectivity. It has been argued that on either plane development is achieved through progressive equilibration. Knowing that any suggestion of parallelism would tempt people to object that there are frequent conflicts between affectivity and intelligence, we have responded in advance. The conflicts in question were not denied, but it was pointed out that they are always conflicts between elements of different levels, e.g. between a mental operation of one level and a feeling of a lower level. With reference to such conflicts, therefore, it is legitimate to speak of regression, but only if this notion, popularized by psychoanalysts and so often criticized since, is not taken literally.

We began with the hypothesis that affectivity can cause accelerations and retardations in the development of intelligence, that it can disturb intellectual functioning and modify its contents, but that it can neither engender nor modify structures. As early as the fifth or even the fourth stage, however, "affective structures" were encountered. These included seriated scales of interests and values involving symmetrical and asymmetrical relations; moral feelings something like operatory rules of affectivity; and the will, which we described as a regulation of regulations analogous to reversible operations. The existence of these structures contradicted, or at least seemed to contradict, the third part of our hypothesis. We resolved the paradox by recognizing that while there is no doubt that affective structures are isomorphic with cognitive structures, they are not a special and separate sort of structure that is different in kind from intellectual structures. In effect, affective structures have to do with an intellectualization of the affective aspect of our exchanges with other people. While at lower levels values result simply from projecting feelings onto objects, at the level of interpersonal exchanges the expression of values in the form of value judgments is an intellectualized expression. A second instance of this intellectualization of feeling is evident in our demonstration that schemes arising from interpersonal relationships are subsequently internalized and applied by the individual to himself.

The term "intellectualization," we have said, has two senses and must be employed with caution. First, it can be taken to mean an action of intelligence on affectivity. We have argued that such an "intellectualist" conception is unintelligible. For our part, we insist upon the heterogeneity of affectivity and intelligence. We can no more accept that there is a formative or modifying action of intelligence on affectivity than that there is such an action of affectivity on intelligence. We prefer, therefore, to interpret intellectualization in its second sense. Under that definition, affective structures become *the cognitive aspect of relationships with other people.*

The dichotomy usually envisioned between intelligence and affectivity is based on the idea that these two aspects of behavior are distinct but analogous mental faculties acting on each other. We reject this conception because, in our view, it creates false problems. It is convenient, but it does not correspond to reality. Behavior cannot be classified under affective and cognitive rubrics. If a distinction must be made, and it appears one should, it would be more accurate to make it between *behaviors related to objects and behaviors related to people.* Both have structural or cognitive and energetic or affective aspects. In behaviors related to objects, the structural aspects are the various empirical and logicomathematical knowledge structures while the energetic aspects are the interests, efforts, and intra-individual feelings that regulate behavior. In behaviors related to people, the energetic element is made up of interpersonal feelings. Ordinarily, these are emphasized exclusively. They contain a structural element, however, which comes from taking consciousness of interpersonal relationships and leads, among other things, to the constitution of value structures. By making the basic distinction between structure and functioning or between structural and energetic aspects of behavior, we believe we have removed the ambiguities that previously existed between affectivity in the broad sense and feelings in the narrow sense of well-defined behavior. At the same time, we believe we have explained the true relationship between intelligence and affectivity in the course of development by avoiding the twin stumbling-blocks of intellectualism and "affective primacy."

SUBJECT INDEX

A

Acquired feelings
  as second stage, 21–25
Activity
  and affectivity
    in second stage
      development, 23
Adaptation
  definition of, 3–4
Adolescence
  and idealistic feelings, 69–72
Affective behavior
  vs cognitive
    definitions, 2–3
Affective decentration
  and object choice, 36–43
Affective function
  vs cognitive function, 6–11
    notion of structure, 9–11
    three theories of conduct,
      7–9
Aggression
  and defense instincts, 17–18
Alimentary instinct
  as hereditary organization,
    17
Altruism
  and selfish behavior
    and interpersonal feelings,
      45
Assimilation
  and accommodation
    definitions, 4–5
Attachment
  to the mother
    and object choice, 37
Autonomous feelings
  and normative affects
    in fifth stage, 65–68
Aversive reactions
  and defense instincts, 17

B

Behavioral regulation
  in third stage development,
    26–43

C

Causality
  and affective decentration, 40
Circular reaction
  and perceptual affects
    in second stage
      development, 23–24
Coenesthesis
  and personality development,
    71

Cognitive behavior
  vs affective behavior
    definitions and concepts,
      2–3
Cognitive decentration
  and object choice, 39–40
Concrete operations
  and normative affects, 14
    structures during, 10
Conflict
  and will exercise
    in fifth stage, 61, 63
Conservation
  of feeling, 13
    and mental operations, 59–60
  of values
    in fifth developmental
      stage, 60–61, 65
Context
  of drives and instincts, 17, 20
Curiosity
  as instinct, 18

D

Decentration
  and will as regulator, 63–64
Defense instincts
  as hereditary organization,
    17–18
Development
  stages of
    overview, 12–15
Developmental retardation
  and hospitalism, 42

E

Effort
  feeling of
    as activation, 28
Emotion
  as form of behavior, 29
Energetics
  and structure, 9–10, 12
Equilibrium
  vs disequilibrium
    and adaptation, 4
  and feeling regulation, 30,
    32–34

F

Fear
  and aggression
    and defense instincts,
      17–18
  in children
    and instinct vs learning,
      16–17

in infants
  and perceptual
    discrimination, 3
First acquired feelings
  as developmental stage, 14,
    21–25
Formal operations
  and idealistic feelings, 14,
    69–72
Formal thought level
  structures during, 10
Freud's theory
  of moral feeling development,
    40
  of object choice, 36–42

G

Games
  rules of
    and normative affects,
      65–66
Gestalt theory
  of need and equilibrium
    in behavior regulation,
      34–36
  and perception definition, 4,
    9
  and sensation/perception
    difference, 22–23
Gratitude
  and conservation of values,
    60

H

Hereditary organizations
  as developmental stage, 14,
    16–20
Hunting instinct
  as hereditary organization,
    17

I

Idealistic feelings
  and formal operations, 14,
    69–72
Illusion
  of over-estimation
    affective aspects of, 7
Imitation
  and object choice, 40–41
  and self-consciousness, 52–54
Inferiority
  feelings of
    and self-estimation, 47–49
Innate Releasing Mechanisms
  and cognitive/affective
    relationship, 3

Instinct
  as hereditary organization,
    16–20
Intelligence
  abstract
    vs affective behavior, 3
  and affectivity
    general conclusions, 73–74
Intelligent acts
  and affect regulation, 26–43
Intentional behavior
  affects regulating
    in third stage development,
      26–43
Interest
  and value
    in behavior regulation, 27,
      31–36
Interpersonal feelings
  first development of, 36
  and intuitive affects, 44–58
Intuitive affects
  and preoperational
    representations, 14
  and social feelings, 44–58

J

Janet's theory
  of behavioral regulations,
    26–30
  critique of, 30–31
Justice
  and conservation of values,
    60, 65–66

L

Language acquisition
  and social instincts, 19
  and stage differentiation,
    14–15
Learning
  role in instincts, 16–19
Lies
  children's reactions to
    and moral feeling
      development, 55–57
Liking
  and disliking
    in fifth stage, 60
    in fourth stage, 44–45
  and moral feeling
    development, 32

M

Mathematical operations
  affective aspects of, 6
Maturation
  as instinct activator, 16

Measuring
  over-estimation experiments
    affective aspects of, 7
Moral feelings
  as affective structures, 73
  and autonomous feelings
    development, 66
  beginning of
    in fourth stage, 49–58
  as normative feeling stage, 13
  origins of, 47
  and valuations, 32, 41
Moral realism
  and seminormative feelings,
    56, 58

N

Narcissism
  criticism of concept, 38
Need
  and equilibrium
    in behavior regulation,
      32–35
Normative affects
  and concrete operations, 14
  as fifth stage, 59–68

O

Obedience
  and autonomous feelings,
    66–67
  and respect
    and moral feeling
      development, 52–55
Object choice
  and affective decentration,
    36–42
Obligation
  and moral feeling
    development, 53
Operations stage
  and normative affects, 59–68

P

Pain
  as affective impression, 22
Parental instincts
  as hereditary organization,
    18–19
Perception
  affective aspects of, 6–8
  and cognitive/affective
    relationship, 3
Perceptual affects
  and first acquired feelings,
    21–25
Perceptual experience
  conflicts with logical
    deduction
    and will regulation, 63

Personality
  formation of
    and idealistic feelings,
      69–72
Personality theories
  of the will, 62
Play instinct
  criticism of concept, 19
Pleasure
  as affective impression, 22
Preoperational level
  structures during, 10
Preoperational representations
  and intuitive affects, 14
Preoperational thought
  and seminormative feeling
    development, 55–56
Psychoanalytic theory
  of feeling construction, 13
Punishment
  child's reaction to
    and moral feeling
      development, 58

R

Reciprocity
  and development of
    interpersonal feelings,
      46–47
  moral
    and autonomous feelings,
      65–68
Reflex mechanisms
  defense instincts as, 17
Representation
  and language
    and interpersonal feelings
      development, 44
Repression
  Freudian concept of
    and affective decentration,
      37–38
Respect
  mutual
    and autonomous feelings
      development, 66–68
  and obedience
    and moral feeling
      development, 52–55
Responsibility
  and moral realism
    and seminormative feeling
      development, 56–57
Rhythm
  of affective life, 21–22

S

Schemes
  interpersonal
    development of, 51–52

Self
  vs personality
    in sixth stage, 71
Self-consciousness
  and behavioral regulation,
    28, 41
  and moral feeling
    development, 52–53
Self-esteem
  and social behavior, 49
Self-estimation
  and interpersonal feelings,
    47–49
Selfish instincts
  criticism of concept, 19
Seminormative feelings
  and moral feeling
    development, 55–58
Sensorimotor intelligence
  affects regulating intentional
    behavior, 26–43
  as developmental stage, 14
  role of emotion during,
    1–2
Seriation
  affective aspects of, 6
Sexual instincts
  and cognitive/affective
    relationship, 3
  as hereditary organization,
    18
Social instincts
  as hereditary organization,
    19

Social learning
  and instinct, 16–19
Social pressure
  and mutual respect, 67–68
Sociological theory
  of the will, 62
Spatiotemporal structure
  of value regulation
    in gestalt theory, 36
Stages
  of intellectual and affective
    development, 12–15
  table of, 14
Structure
  and energetics, 7–10, 12
Success
  and failure
    influence on behavior,
      48–49
Superiority
  feelings of
    and self-estimation, 47–49
Symbolic function
  and interpersonal feeling
    development, 44

T

Truthfulness
  and conservatipn of values,
    60, 66
  see also Lies

V

Value
  and interest
    in behavior regulation,
      27, 31–36, 42–43
Values
  and affective structures,
    73–74
  conservation of
    in fifth stage, 59–61, 65
Verbal intelligence
  as developmental stage,
    14
  and intuitive affects, 44–58

W

Will
  as affective structure, 73
  and conflict between drives,
    13, 15
  included in affectivity, 2
  problem of
    in fifth stage, 61–63
  as regulation of regulations
    in fifth stage, 63–65
Worry
  as precautionary behavior,
    29